THE CHIAROSCURO MARKET

THE CHIAROSCURO MARKET

ART THEFT AND THE ART WORLD

by

KEMPTON MOONY

FKM BOOKS

New York

CONTENTS

Introduction

The following is an examination of the phenomenon of art theft and the establishment of the art theft community in the twentieth century western world. Every year thousands of art thefts are reported, with potentially just as many going unreported. In 1999, 24,598 works of art and antiques were stolen in Italy alone.[1] Some of these works were recovered, while others have been distributed through channels they otherwise would not have traveled. In this way, art theft alters the circles in which a work of art circulates. Many victims view art thefts as simply frustrating events and desire to make them pass as quickly and quietly as possible. However, this does little to help understand art theft and deal with its consequences. What I propose is an understanding of the art world in a relationship with the art theft community, with each significantly affecting the other.

I should clarify what I mean by the "art theft community." I do not intend to suggest that every art thief is in close association with all other art thieves. Instead, this work will draw out a number of different types of theft that can involve any number of players. Both simple and elaborate networks are used to transport stolen art, and

---

[1] Interpol, 2002, *Statistics of Stolen Cultural Property: Objects,* 1999 ed., Available [Online]: <http://www.interpol.com> [February 10, 2002].

there are similar networks used to sell stolen art. By looking at the multitude of small and large networks as one
collective, loose community, united through patterns of
interaction, of motivation, and of consequences, we can
study how this collective community interacts with the legitimate art world. It is this legitimate art world that forms
the largest and most complex connection between art
thieves.

To understand art theft, it is necessary to be clear
what is meant by the word "art." When I use the terms
"art object" or "work of art," I will be restricting myself to
the visual fine arts, referring to a physical object that is
considered by a group to be inspired and of great importance to their well-being and culture.[2] The core of this, for
the purposes of this paper, consists of paintings, drawings,
and sculpture held in art museums, galleries, and collections. The importance placed on an art object by a group
gives it a value for which it can be bought and sold, making the art object a commodity.

Though this paper will focus specifically on art theft,
art theft is inextricably tied with art fraud, forgery, and the
faking of provenances of artworks. These topics will be
discussed to the extent that they clarify how art theft operates in society. Also, the history of art theft is tied to looting during wartime, the looting of archeological sites, and
the illicit trade of antiquities. While there are many similarities and connections, these activities manifest themselves in different kinds of distribution networks and have
their own distinct complexities, and so will be discussed
only so far as they help in the understanding of art theft.
There have also been a great deal of stories about art theft
in popular culture, including films, fictional books, and
other media. This thematic popularity of art theft will be
briefly discussed to show the results of art theft on the general public, but this paper will focus on the effects of actual
incidences of art theft as distinct from fictional incidences.

There has been little scholarship written on art theft as
different from archaeological looting and antiquities smuggling. Art theft has only been examined empirically by
four authors. The first study of art theft was conducted by

---

[2] *Art History and Its Methods*, ed. Eric Fernie (London:
Phaidon, 1998), 326.

Bonnie Burnham in her text *The Art Crisis*, which came from her work on the International Council of Museums on the topic of ethical acquisitions. She split her focus between what she calls the art crisis and the antiquities crisis, arguing that as prices of both art and antique objects have risen, "their function as art has diminished."[3] J. Barelli in his dissertation *On the Business of Art and Antique Theft* studies art and antique theft in England, focusing on the organization and work of Scotland Yard's art theft squad.[4] He also interviews several art thieves and concludes that if a thief has connections with art dealers, disposing of stolen art is relatively easy and profitable. Truc-Nhu Thi Ho's dissertation *Art Theft in New York City* focuses on gallery thieves who steal for profit.[5] In his text, he develops qualitative models of decision-making in art theft. His information comes from a survey of gallery owners in New York who were questioned about thefts from their collections. Finally, there is Robert Middlemas's *The Double Market*, which focuses on the development of the black market in art and describes the techniques of various kinds of art thieves.[6]

In addition to these texts there are is John Conklin's *Art Crime,* which draws heavily from Burnham, but spreads its scope to cover forgeries, art fraud, vandalism, and gives recommendations for curbing these phenomenon.[7] There are also a number of texts recounting entertaining stories of art theft, including Milton Esterow's *Art Stealers*, Hugh McLeave's *Rogues in the Gallery*, and Robert Wraight's *The Art Game*.

Here I will sew together and expand the ideas by these authors. I will examine the phenomenon of art theft in the western art market to demonstrate how the inner-workings

---

[3] Bonnie Burnham, *The Art Crisis* (New York: St. Martin's Press, 1975), 14.

[4]   J. Barelli, *On the Business of Art and Antique Theft*, Diss., Fordham University, 1986, 2.

[5] Truc-Nhu Thi Ho, *Art Theft in New York City: An Exploratory Study in Crime Specificity*, Diss., Rutgers University, 1992, 1.

[6] Robert Middlemas, *The Double Market: Art Theft and Art Thieves* (Farnborough: Saxon House, 1975), 1.

[7] John Conklin, *Art Crime* (London: Praeger, 1994), 3.

of the black market and legal market affect each other in such a way that there is not always a definitive line between the two. I will examine the motives of those involved in the black market, particularly those motives related to characteristics of the legitimate art world to reveal the way it acts upon the art theft community. And I will examine the repercussions of art theft on various groups, including those in the legitimate art world to show how it is influenced by the art theft community. These latter two parts should reinforce the intertwined nature of the black market and the legal market.

We will begin with a brief history of art theft to give the roots of the phenomenon and how it increased throughout the 1960s. This will be followed by a section describing the various characters involved in art thefts to explain how different kinds of thefts take place. After this, these characters' various motives and then the consequences of their actions will be explored. A series of interviews of art dealers I conducted will come next to show how specific people are affected by the art theft community. The final section will discuss these motives and consequences in terms of the way art theft add to the construction of art's value. Through these descriptions, I hope to illuminate an integral part of the art market which, though it has been used to entertain the public, has received little attention from art historians.

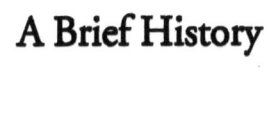
A Brief History

Before 1961

Though there have always been art thefts, modern art theft has its roots in acts of wartime looting. After successful battles throughout Europe, Napoleon would loot the defeated areas for masterpieces, such as the *Apollo Belvedere* and the *Laocoon Group*, and bring them to Paris. He wished to transform Paris into the new center of world culture, a view summed up by Napoleon's Lt. Barbier who, taking charge of a shipment of goods in Holland, is recorded as saying, "Too long have these masterpieces been sullied by the gazes of the serfs."[8] Not only did the act demonstrate the superior might of the goods' new owners, but it also demonstrated Napoleon's belief that the works would find an audience in Paris more able to appreciate fine art. The great cultural fertilization of Paris was believed to help its artists mature, so that the talent of French painters would in a matter of years exceed that of Italian Renaissance artists. Court painters were treated like royalty, with many of their pictures going straight into museums. This attested to the greatness of the French painters and the subjects they depicted, such as Napoleon himself, but it also robbed those who admired the paintings of a chance of buying the works.

---

[8] Middlemas, 5.

Before Napoleon, wartime looting had been conducted mostly by soldiers on a random basis. Napoleon's treasure hunting, however, was systematically performed, with high figures like Josephine Bonaparte taking works for themselves.[9] Following France's defeat in 1814, most of the plunder was returned, despite Stendhal's claim that France had acquired the artworks by treaty, but the Allies had confiscated it without a treaty.[10] Repatriation was eased by the fact that the loot was housed in museums and the provenances of the works were well known. A hundred years later, Hitler would remember this repatriation.

Napoleon's tactics of building a European cultural center were carefully studied by Hitler, whose fetishistic belief in the power of simple objects would lead him to conduct a materialist cultural cleansing that would supplement his ethnic genocide. He believed that the wrong art could infect and pervert a healthy populace, while the right art could act as a kind of enlightenment pill, educating the German masses and raising them spiritually. Taking from Napoleon's vision of Paris, he sought to make his hometown of Linz the new center of world culture. The result was what Lynn Nicholas has called the "Rape of Europa;" the greatest works of art were aggressively looted from all over Europe to fill a national collection that would be the envy of every country.[11] Works that were labeled degenerate, or which did not fit the national agenda, were disposed of, sometimes destroyed, with Hitler's aesthetic taste reigning supreme. Late in the war when his armies were retreating, Hitler consciously decided to hide and destroy much of this vast collection of looted masterpieces rather than let the works be repatriated. He believed the works were the rightful property of the German people and could not tolerate the idea of the works leaving Germany. Luckily, allied forces found many of his caches before his orders of destruction were carried out.[12]

---

[9] Conklin, 218.

[10] Ibid.

[11] Lynn H. Nicholas, *The Rape of Europa* (New York: Alfred A. Knopf, 1994).

[12] Milton Esterow, *Art Stealers* (New York: Macmillan, 1973), 105.

The German occupation had another side effect on the art world. The prices that had been steadily climbing in the first part of the century dropped and would not rise through the 1930s and early 1940s. A glut had developed in the art market as many Europeans were forced to liquidate their assets and flee their homes. The sudden glut made selling artworks difficult, and would later make tracing the provenances of works difficult.

The post-war art market developed in a haphazard fashion due to the different ways various countries were touched by the war. Under currency restrictions, English art dealers had difficulty buying antiques in Europe and French dealers could not easily buy works in England. The war had produced among some a xenophobia, with collectors hoarding works that came from their own cultural heritage. In Germany there was a demand for pewter tankards and hunting paraphernalia, which were seen as traditional, German objects. The demand resulted in a series of thefts, but little concern was shown by the police as the objects were small and ordinary.[13]

Usually, the demand for German antiques was satisfied by legal means until small, wooden religious statues came to be sought after by emerging industrialists. Over the centuries, a number of these had passed into secular hands, with many being sold "quasi-legally" by churches or looted in the post-1945 confusion, but this was not enough to satisfy the demand.[14] Forgers tried to fill the demand for the statues by carving replicas from the timbers of old houses, but thieves could more easily rob the shrines of small Bavarian towns. These shrines were usually left unlocked and open, making them easy targets for a trend of thefts that would grow until 1961. Industrialists in Dusseldorf and Essen were not concerned with the statues' original contexts and the religious connotations of the statues were transformed into connotations of wealth and status. In the beginning, authorities made little efforts to prevent these thefts. Police records concerning the theft of antiquities were such a mess that even as of 1965, hoards

---

[13] Middlemas, 35.
[14] Ibid., 36.

of statues were being found that had never been recorded as stolen.[15]

At the same time, similar vogues for traditional decorative objects developed in Italy and Austria, and by 1955, in France and Belgium. Black market dealers and those who made their living during World War II by scrounging hard to acquire items found outlets for their abilities in the civilian world. Italian organizers of theft rings included art dealers who had previously been employed by Hitler's top art vulture Hermann Goering. Goering, who attained the posts of head of the Luftwaffe, director of the Four Year Plan, and simultaneously the Prime Minister of Prussia, was a greedy collector, particularly of baroque art, and his character is exemplified by his use of his collection. He used Rubens's *Diana at the Stag Hunt* as the cover for his movie screen.[16] It had been Goering who had ordered the close of the Bauhaus in 1933 and developed the idea of selling pictures Nazi tastes found undesirable to other countries to support military funds.

Not everyone connected with the black market had these kinds of associations. In 1961, it was found that two priests, Fathers Guido Martinelli and Alessandro Vasco, had taken over 400 items from the church of San Felipo Neri in Naples. The pieces they had taken were laundered and smuggled into various Italian state galleries, showing the chaotic state of Italy's Ministry of Fine Arts. Most of the works were never recovered, but despite this, the two fathers were described as saints, not thieves, by locals as the two had never personally profited from the sales. Instead, Martinelli and Vasco used the sales to help pay for the upkeep of their church and donated some of the proceeds to the poor during a time that was economically difficult.[17] Under Italian patrimony laws, it was illegal for the church to sell its property; however, the two priests were released.

Across the Atlantic, America offered a developing market for international distributers of stolen works, though it too was subject to thefts. As early as 1952, a church in a Kentucky town was relieved of nine works including ones attributed to Rubens, Murillo, and van Eyck.

---

[15] Ibid., 38.
[16] Nicholas, 40.
[17] McLeave, 173-4.

Town legend had it that Louis Philippe, before becoming King of France, had fallen ill traveling to New Orleans and had recovered in the town. When he returned to France, he had sent the paintings with some other gifts in appreciation of the town's kindness towards him.[18] The theft of these paintings was the start of a wave of art thefts in the mid-1950s that journalists would describe as "incomprehensible."[19]

The increasing thefts meant more awareness of the problem and more attention given to it by authorities. But the art theft community was quick to adapt. In 1959, two years after one theft had caused it to install alarms, the Toronto Art Gallery lost $1.5 million worth of paintings in a second theft, including a Hals, a Rembrandt, a Renoir, and a Rubens. Rumors began that the works were being held until the insurance companies paid a ransom demand. Toronto police refused to comment, though subsequent evidence supports the view that a ransom was paid.

Two years later, on the fiftieth anniversary of the theft of the *Mona Lisa*, a portrait of the Duke of Wellington by Goya was stolen from the National Gallery in London. The piece was to be returned if the elderly of England would be excused from a television tax.[20] By ransoming the artwork, the thief, Kempton Bunton, did not have to concern himself with smuggling, faking provenances, or finding a buyer. Once ransoming was established by this and the Toronto case, it became a popular form of art theft, particularly for political purposes.

---

[18] The nine paintings were recovered, however during the ensuing trial of those who were caught with four of the works, the attributions of the Rubens, Murillo and van Eyck were highly contested. Though no consensus was arrived at, the church continues to value the paintings as the greatest of masterpieces. Esterow 202.

[19] Middlemas, 43.

[20] Esterow, 18.

After 1961

The year of the Goya theft, 1961, was a dividing line; it became apparent, if it had not been already, that art theft was an international problem of tremendous scale. The trend spread into India and Japan, and there was a remarkable series of thefts on the French Riviera that would last several years as a result of the French Ministry of Cultural Affairs striking a bargain with ransomers. Italian police made only one recovery in 1961.[21] Stories about recovery were talked about less due to fears of promoting more thefts as prices for art rose rapidly each year.[22] In 1957, the most expensive painting sold was the *Merode Triptych* by the Master of Flemalle, sold for £303,500. In 1959, it was Vermeer's *Portrait of a Young Woman* for £400,000, in 1961, it was Rembrandt's *Aristotle contemplating a Bust of Homer* for £821,000, and in 1970, Velazquez's *Juan de Pareja* sold for £2,310,000.[23] The boom in the art market would last through 1969, during which time this atmosphere would help art theft to grow.

The mid-1960s saw the western world wake up to the problem of art theft and this led to the restructuring of re-

---

[21] McLeave, 61.

[22] Solomon R. Guggenheim Foundation v. Lubell, 550 NYS 2d 618 NY Super. Ct. 1990.

[23] Peter Watson, *From Manet to Manhattan* (New York, Random House, 1992), 485.

covery organizations, the concentration of resources used for recovery, and international cooperation in sharing information about trafficking. The circulation of information was realized to be vital if works that were smuggled out of a country were to be recovered. This involved the circulation of notices about thefts internationally among police as well as dealers, auction houses, galleries, and museums. However, the circulation of these notices was, and still is, frowned upon by many as the public airing of an institution's problems.

The restructuring of the counterattack against art theft led criminals to rethink their strategies. In this, the case of T. Edward Hanley set a precedent. In 1968, Hanley was robbed of over a million dollars' worth of modern paintings. To recover the works, his wife offered a reward for their return and a week later the pictures were recovered and no arrests were made. This slight change was the result of changing legislation meant to deter ransoming. In Britain in 1968, laws relating to theft were tightened, while at the same time, the old common-law of compounding a felony was abolished. An accomplice in a crime could no longer be charged with a serious offense if he gave information that led to the recovery of stolen property. The new laws reflected insurance companies' claims adjusters placing more importance on recovering works and minimizing losses than on the prosecution of guilty parties. And when faced with the choice of recovering their collection or catching the culprit responsible, most collectors chose to recover their collection. So began the trend of stealing art for a reward, a slight variation of stealing for a ransom.

The climbing prices of the art market paused briefly in 1969, but the market began to pick up again in 1971 and prices in art spiraled higher than any other commodity.[24] The revival suggested that art could be a secure investment and the highly publicized situation was bursting with opportunities for art theft. The amount of artworks that was changing hands made it difficult to keep track of who owned what and where. Many works were being stored in warehouses where they would not be missed for

---

[24] Middlemas, 52.

months, sometimes years, if they were taken.[25] Pieces that were stolen could have provenances faked, they could be laundered through a series of owners, disguised by a restorer to alter the look of a work, or hidden somewhere out of sight until the heat passed.[26] While America had little problem with the illegal exporting of art objects, it had become a point of redistribution. As one British dealer of the time noted, "Once stuff is across the Atlantic, no questions are asked by many dealers. They are only too happy to have the stuff to sell."[27]

Whether the artwork is stolen to collect a reward, to be ransomed, to be sold through a network of dealers, or to be kept as a personal possession, all those who are involved in art theft can be divided into two categories. They either seek to obtain and keep a work of art to possess or to capitalize on a work by holding it for a short time before sending it elsewhere. These two types of participants are the nodes which direct stolen art and which constitute the stolen art community. In the next section, this community will be divided up in terms of various kinds of theft to explore how the need to possess a work of art is transformed into an act of theft.

---

[25] Solomon R. Guggenheim Foundation v. Lubell.
[26] Burnham, 47.
[27] Middlemas, 59.

Ingredients for a Theft

Clearly, the success of an art theft depends, to a large extent, on there being a favorable opportunity for a theft. John Conklin divides the components that determine a favorable opportunity into three categories: artwork that is suitable to be stolen, a lack of security, and the presence of people motivated to steal a work.[28]

A work's suitability to be stolen is largely the degree to which it can be easily moved physically and easily marketed. As Mark Twain once said, "How easy it is to steal a white elephant but how hard it is to get rid of it."[29] A well known work that demands a high price is easily identifiable and hard to sell unless a patron has commissioned the piece to be stolen. Unknown works are easily sold to naive buyers, but many of them must be stolen to bring in a profit worth the risk of the theft. Most stolen works are slightly lesser known works or works by second-tier masters, as fewer buyers are likely to recognize these from descriptive notices distributed by authorities and the theft is less likely to receive wide media attention.

One example is the theft of *Frost Flowers, Ipswich 1889* by Arthur Wesley Dow. The painting had been donated to the University of California, Los Angeles, but

[28] Conklin, 119.
[29] Esterow, 246.

was taken by employee Jane Crawford after one of her coworkers told her the work was valuable. According to Los Angeles Police Department files, Crawford asked two associates of hers to find a buyer for the painting, and asked for one, who was a painter, to paint a forgery of the painting which she used to disguise the paintings theft.[30] Her associates contacted an agent who in turn contacted the Ira Spanierman Gallery in New York. Spanierman bought the painting for $200, 000, had it restored, and sold it to a buyer for $317,000. Each of these sources failed to research the ownership of the painting to sufficiently assure themselves that the work was not stolen. Crawford then laundered the money obtained from the sale of the Dow so that her name was not on any transaction papers. After her initial success, Crawford targeted eight more paintings, each which she handled in the same manner. Crawford came under suspicion only after a falling out with her associates, who turned her in after striking deals with authorities. The case was complicated by the Spanierman Gallery, "who initially stonewalled the investigation, refusing to cooperate with detectives to determine whether the gallery had purchased a stolen painting."[31] The Dow was able to fetch a substantial price, but was not a piece that was well enough known to so as it was easily recognizable.

Security will deter many thefts, however, many owners of art, such as churches, small dealers, and small collectors, are unable to afford security. Others believe that viewers will be too awed by the aura of an artwork to steal it. And some complain how the presence of security alters the viewing of art. Bonnie Burnham believes that the presence of security contributes to art thefts as it often stifles the environment in which a work is shown. A display can distort a work behind protective glass. Unable to enjoy the work in its context, a viewer may wish to take the work to a more suitable setting.[32] This viewer desires to relate to art

---

[30] Los Angeles Police Department, 2002, *Art Theft Case Files: Hidden Treasure*, 2000 ed., Available [Online]: <http://www.lapdonline.org/get_involved/stolen_art/cases/treasure.htm> [April 20, 2002].
[31] Ibid.
[32] Ibid., 14.

but is frustrated by the context in which the art is located, and this frustration results in an aggressive act. However, it is also possible that the increase in security and the increase in art theft are two parallel, but independent events. On the other hand, some thieves have justified thefts from places with low security by describing the work as neglected and not properly protected.[33] No matter what the security, the history of art theft has proven that if someone wants a work bad enough, they will find a way to take it. For this reason, officials are reluctant to discuss their security measures for fear of displaying vulnerable points.

Many times, museums have refused to admit to being robbed, and have not even reported thefts to the police, instead taking matters into their own hands to keep the situation quiet, to avoid poor publicity, and to avoid encouraging future thefts. The theft of a Chagall gouache which was stolen from the Solomon R. Guggenheim Foundation is an example.[34] The work was stolen sometime in the mid-1960s and the Guggenheim Foundation in court claimed that they decided not to report the work as stolen, "in the belief, not uncommon in the 1960s and 1970s, that to do so would not help to locate the gouache and might hinder its recovery by driving it further underground."[35] Jules Lubell bought the work in 1967 from "a reputable Manhattan gallery ... without knowledge of any defects in the gallery's title."[36] The Guggenheim Foundation had contacted Chagall and the cataloguer of his works, Franz Meyer, and both were consulted by Lubell before the purchase of the work, but this was not enough to notify the Guggenheim Foundation of the location of its painting before the statute of limitations on its ownership expired. The case demonstrates how difficult it can be to determine that a painting is a stolen work of art and how difficult the victim's choice of action can be. Both parties did what they believed was proper, but the problem of art theft is not so easily solved. There is also no guarantee that reporting the theft to the police would have helped the Guggenheim Foundation as no means of curb-

---

[33] Conklin, 168.
[34] Solomon R. Guggenheim Foundation v. Lubell.
[35] Ibid.
[36] Ibid.

ing art theft is completely effective. Cases such as these illustrate why so many art theft cases go unsolved.

The most essential ingredient for a theft is the motivated offender and whether he decides the theft is worth the risk. One factor is the likelihood of being apprehended; many thieves are attracted to art theft as approximately only 20% of art theft cases are solved.[37] This is a vast improvement from 1975, when the chances of recovering a work of art were only 1%.[38] In the case of the stolen Dow, police stated that Crawford would not have been caught but for the falling out with her associates.[39]

The small chances of being apprehended lures many different types of individuals to be involved in art theft and the distribution of stolen works. These include professional thieves with various approaches, receivers who organize thefts and determine the future of the loot, smugglers, disguisers who may forge provenances or alter the appearance of the loot, dealers with varying degrees of knowledge about the sources of the works they peddle, and buyers who also have varying degrees of knowledge about the works they buy. For example, in the New York Supreme Court case of *Porter v. Wertz*, Harold Von Maker, presenting himself as Peter Wertz, took a painting by Utrillo from Samuel Porter, an art dealer, without ever paying Porter.[40] Von Maker, then sold the painting to the Richard Feigen Gallery, who transported the painting to Venezuela. Though it appears that the Feigen Gallery bought the work in good faith, the case is complicated by the gallery's failure to confirm that Von Maker was a legitimate dealer. If someone were to have bought the painting from Feigen, this buyer in all likelihood, would have a difficult time determining that the work was stolen. The work would be reinstated in the legitimate art world, but in a completely different set of circles than its rightful owner.

As the work of art encounters dealers and buyers who are less aware that it is stolen, it progresses into the legitimate art world, resulting in an intermingling of the illegit-

[37] Ibid., 129.
[38] Middlemas, 170.
[39] Los Angeles Police Department.
[40] Porter v. Wertz, 26 UCC 876 NY Super. Ct. 1979.

imate and the legitimate art worlds. The number of people involved depends upon the type of theft. These types of theft include connoisseur theft, commissioned theft for collectors, theft for sale to a dishonest dealer, theft to be consigned to an auction house, for ransom, and for political purposes.

Types of Theft

Connoisseur theft, or theft for personal possession, usually involves only one person. Etoh Mvondo, a twenty year old from Paris, took three paintings, including a Renoir, from three different French museums in 1990. He received three years in prison after explaining that he was building his own collection. "I'm a lover of art. The idea of owning a Renoir at the age of twenty fascinated me."[41] Another example is Louis Hillen, a painter who stole nine artworks and displayed them in his New York apartment with special mounts and lights. He explained to the authorities that the prices of the works were not important and that he had taken the works from galleries in SoHo because he liked them and they were easy to take.[42] Here, the work of art appeals to someone to such a degree that possessing it is worth the consequences of being caught with the work. Because the work was stolen to be possessed, it usually will not return to the open market, affecting the art world in a different way than works stolen to be sold.

Theft for commission is similar to connoisseur theft, but involves more people. When a Cezanne painting worth £3 million was stolen from an Oxford museum, Su-

---

[41] Conklin, 132.
[42] Ibid., 132.

perintendent John Carr of Oxford Police said, "Whoever has taken this painting has given some thought to how to steal it.... The person has some reason for it and some outlet for it."[43] Police also believed that the painting was "'stolen to order' by drugs gangs or arms dealers who use works to launder money."[44] Procedures such as these involve forethought, which connoisseur theft may or may not involve, offenders often times taking a piece impulsively.

A slightly different variation on this theme is a dealer commissioning a theft. In 1984, a Boston art dealer was convicted of conspiracy, transporting, and receiving stolen property. A hired burglar testified that the dealer had described the types of paintings he desired: French and Dutch paintings of small size, scenes with people rather than animals or portraits, and no paintings with ships or American flags.[45] Pictures fitting this description would be hard to identify and be popular among the dealer's clientele. Some dealers are reported to have supplied thieves with shopping lists, such as a museum or gallery catalog, some dealers may simply buy what they know to be stolen works, and some may simply be lax in researching a work's ownership.[46] Such was the case in Crawford's theft of the Dow. The work may be bought from a thief directly, from a receiver, or another dealer, as the more hands a work passes through, the more its original ownership becomes blurred.

Over the years, channels have developed for stolen works to pass through. Certain unscrupulous dealers know thieves and smugglers who can do what they want done. Sometimes, if a dealer cannot sell works, he will pay for these works to be stolen so he can collect on an insurance policy. This was the case in a 1986 burglary of the Re-

---

[43] BBC News, 2002, *Hunt for Stolen Cezanne*, January 1, 2000 ed., Available [Online]: <http://news.bbc.co.uk/hi/english/uk/newsid_586000/586834.stm> [April 20, 2002].
[44] BBC News, 2002, *The Art of Art Theft*, January 1, 2000 ed., Available [Online]: <http://news.bbc.co.uk/hi/english/uk/newsid_587000/587183.stm> [April 20, 2002].
[45] Conklin, 137.
[46] Burnham, 42.

gency World Wide Packing warehouse in New York.[47] In court, Houshang Mahboubian and his accomplices were found to have entered into a conspiracy to stage a burglary of Mahboubian's collection. Several art experts testified that a number of the pieces in the collection were of dubious authenticity. From the testimony of other witnesses, the court concluded that Mahboubian had become aware of this before the burglary and had been unsuccessful in selling his collection. Mahboubian had insured his collection with Lloyd's of London for $18.5 million, covering it in transit, and had then conspired with two other men to burgle the collection while at a transit stop in New York. One of these men, Abe Garabedian, then

> ...in turn spoke to several men experienced in robberies and burglaries of art storage facilities. Garabedian told them that Sakhai had "an insurance job" for them. Unbeknownst to the others, one of the men -- Daniel Cardebat -- had agreed to act as a police informant, and secretly recorded all of their conversations.[48]

This case demonstrates how the art theft community has become an organized business operation that has found a home under the disguise of legal trade. Criminals such as Mahboubian require others in the art world to be continuously suspicious of what they look at so as not to be taken in.

In time, even experts forget what stolen works look like; in an experiment by the television show "60 Minutes," the director of the Art Institute of Chicago was unable to identify a Cezanne painting that had been stolen from his museum less than a year before.[49] The knowledge of this makes refusing good deals on stolen works hard for some dealers to resist, as well as the knowledge that if they do not purchase the work, another dealer will.

Many auction houses are guilty of not checking the backgrounds of works, and so it is common for recently

---

[47] People v. Mahboubian, 544 NYS 2d 769 NY Ct. of Appeals 1989.
[48] Ibid.
[49] Conklin, 136.

stolen works to be consigned to auction houses. There are two main reasons for doing this. One is to sell the work for more than the 10% of its legitimate value that is the standard on the black market. The second is for the party who put it up for sale to buy it and obtain a legitimate bill of sale. The owners can then place the work in storage and wait for the statute of limitations to expire, at which time the work, stolen or not, should become legal property of anyone who can demonstrate that they bought the work in good faith. A failed example of this is contained in the New York Supreme Court case *Tajan v. Pavia & Harcourt.*[50] In 1981, Enzo Columbo of Florence, Italy, reported stolen, among other works of art, a painting by Bernado Bellotto. An international notice was provided by Interpol in a 1982 art theft bulletin. In 1985, the painting reappeared and was placed for auction with Christie's Inc. in New York. However, before the painting could be sold, the work was seized by the United States Customs Service as requested by letters from the Italian government. Due to the number of lots with which large auction houses like Christie's deal, some objects' history of ownership goes unresearched, as evident in Christie's ignorance of the 1982 art theft bulletin. In its defense against being sued by the DeShong Museum for selling fourteen stolen paintings, Sotheby's Holdings Inc. claimed that it was "impossible to check the titles to all items."[51] Experienced art thieves know and take advantage of this to reintroduce works into the open market.

Some thieves will take a work on the speculation that they will be able to find a buyer. These are usually inexperienced art thieves who do not know the proper channels of distribution and are surprised how little someone will pay them for a work. The Dow theft by Crawford was undertaken on speculation, however in subsequent thefts, she photographed works she planned to steal to investigate interest in them before actually taking the pieces.[52] When a buyer is not readily found for a stolen work, many times the work will be offered back to the owner or the owner's

---

[50] Tajan v. Pavia & Harcourt, 639 NYS 2d 544 NY Super. Ct. 1999.

[51] Conklin, 110.

[52] Los Angeles Police Department.

insurance company for a reward. Other times, the thief may threaten to destroy the work unless some ransom is paid.

The ransoming of a work of art can also be performed for political purposes. As mentioned before, the theft of Goya's *Duke of Wellington* was performed by a man who sought to ease the lives of the elderly in England. Astounded by the amount of money paid for the painting, he sought to correct what he saw as an injustice: a fortune of taxpayers' money paid for a piece of canvas while the government takes money from those who have retired.[53] By "artnapping" a painting, he could hold it hostage until his demands were met, until retirees did not have to pay a television tax. Another more recent case is the 2001 theft of a Chagall from the New York Jewish Museum. Shortly after the piece disappeared, a note was found stating the painting would be held until there was peace in the Middle East. The work was recovered in less than a year with no further explanation yet discovered.[54] As with most cases where the culprits have evaded capture, the thieves' motives are assessed largely in terms of the consequences of their actions. Perhaps the note was made to mislead the police while the thieves attempted to sell the work. Or perhaps the thieves wanted to bring more popular attention to the concurrent Middle Eastern peace talks. The next section will further examine motives like these. By gaining a better understanding of these motives, it is possible not only to shed light on the needs of a few who act outside what is perceived as acceptable, but also on the needs of a larger public whose interaction with art is mirrored as well as affected by art theft.

---

[53] Conklin, 151.
[54] Carol Vogel, "Expert Says Topeka Postal Item Is Stolen Chagall," *New York Times,* February 15, 2002, 43.

Motives

Those Who Pass

As said before, there are two types of characters in the field of art theft. One seeks to possess art in order to pass the work on, using the work as a kind of currency. Crawford's theft of the Dow was such a case. The second seeks to possess art and to retain it, indicating a secondary function for stolen art. As a currency, art can be traded for other commodities, but stolen art is restricted in the way that it can be traded, placing limits upon its value. The value is different for each owner, depending upon their connections in the art world, their knowledge of the art market, and how the work appeals to them personally. A thief who is hired for his skills by a receiver may not know the intricacies of the market and would be unable to sell a work. For this reason, he does not sell it himself, but takes what the receiver offers for it. The receiver with better connections will be able to sell the work for a larger price. The piece may be sold to someone who believes the work to be sold in good standing and pays close to what the work would fetch on the open market by passing the stolen work as legitimate. This is a way in which the open market interacts with the black market. The open market feeds the illicit market by promising a high price paid for illegal activities and by creating an opportunity where this promise can be fulfilled with little fear of prosecution. Or the piece may be sold to someone who knows the work is stolen. This gives the buyer leverage and the ability to ask for a price below what the work would fetch on the open market. The price of the work declines as the buyer perceives a risk of buying a stolen work and therefore a risk of being arrested.

At first this appears relatively simple, but there is another payment that is being paid. The monetary price paid for the work is inversely proportionate to the amount of fear of involvement in an illicit activity that accompanies the work. The connoisseur thief who works alone is held solely responsible for the theft of a work, so while he may not pay any money for the work, he does pay in terms of his peace of mind. He must be constantly aware of his activities so that they do not attract suspicion. In the case of the *Duke of Wellington* theft, Kempton Bunton turned himself in four years after the theft, and six weeks after returning the painting, saying "I didn't want someone to turn me in for the reward. I have let something drop and someone knows I did it."[55] For four years he had lived in fear of letting "something drop" and had to keep his secret from his wife, family, and friends. This was his payment for the work of art.

The effect of stealing an artwork has a parallel with that of a collector buying an artwork. Where the thief fears the police and the ability of the collector to take back the work, the collector fears the thief taking the work. The collector may photograph the work to make it easier to identify if lost, or install an alarm system, or take out an insurance policy. Many times all of these techniques are employed. The thief's behavior is significantly changed by a constant awareness of his potentially being caught, so he keeps secrets, lies, and creates a facade of innocence. The collector's behavior is changed by a constant awareness of the potential loss of the object. The insurance company then capitalizes on this anxiety of being separated from the object.

According to McLeave, 99% of art theft is performed for money.[56] However, art theft is not the only way to

---

[55] Esterow, 18.
[56] McLeave, 121.

make money, and so it is safe to assume that there are other motivating forces at work. It appears too simplistic to reduce 99% of art theft to one motive, when in all probability there are multiple motivations for each theft, as well as many separate needs being satisfied. Certainly an important factor is the likelihood of getting caught. Though the percentage of cases solved has increased from 1% in 1975 to 20% in recent years, this is still considerably less than other types of theft. [57] For example, according to the Texas Department of Public Safety, 74% of the motor vehicles reported stolen in 1999 were recovered.[58] That same year, 39% of all property reported stolen in Texas was recovered, indicating that stolen art is less likely to be recovered than most other types of property.[59] Knowledge of this is likely to make art theft more appealing than other types of theft to potential thieves.

Even when there is a conviction, art's aura of respectability seems to rub off on the hands that steal it as most convictions result in minimal sentencing. Kempton Bunton received three months in prison for admitting to have stolen a work which shortly before the time of its theft in 1961 was bought by London's National Gallery for £140,000. It is doubtful that someone who was convicted for stealing the equivalent amount in cash would receive such a light sentence, even if the culprit had intended the money to go to charity. Vincenzo Perugia was sentenced to seven months in prison for stealing the *Mona Lisa* and exporting it to Italy, and he had no intention of returning the work to France.[60] Instead, he sought to deliver the work to Italy, erroneously believing the work to have been looted from Italy by Napoleon.[61] Here, Napoleon's pillaging is influencing thefts a century later, and in the act of trying to correct what Perugia saw as Napoleon's wrong doings, he committed the same offense which had angered him. As there is no way of placing a price on the

---

[57] Conklin, 129, and Middlemas, 170.
[58] *Crime in Texas:1999* (Austin, TX: Texas Department of Public Safety, 2000), 12.
[59] Ibid.
[60] Robert Wraight, *The Art Game* (New York: Simon and Schuster, 1966), 177.
[61] Ibid.

Mona Lisa, subsequent convicted art thieves have reminded the courts of this case as a precedence for leniency in sentencing. The defense attorney of four men who pleaded guilty to stealing twenty paintings from Saint-Paul-de-Vence in 1960 appealed for leniency by stating, "The Italian who stole the *Mona Lisa* was sentenced to only a year in prison."[62] The prosecution had asked for terms of five to eight years, and the judge compromised, drawing terms of two to three years.[63]

There is something about art that ennobles, if artificially, those who come in contact with it. This is a motivation in itself, as many thieves may be lured by the aura of the art. This is certainly true of connoisseur thieves, like Mvondo and his theft of the Renoir, but even hired thieves may be attracted to an idea of high status they associate with those who handle art. Through their contact with stolen works, they too achieve this status, participating in the art world and interacting with what they view as an important piece of culture. On the other hand, art theft can be an act of revenge against those who normally handle art by someone who feels alienated or envious of them due to their position in society. Some thieves have said they took artworks to embarrass the museum that owned them and to show the way that the works were neglected. In 1939, Serge-Clause Bogousslavsky admitted to stealing Watteau's *L'Indifferent* from the Louvre to correct poor restorations on the work.[64] The French press ridiculed the museum for its indifference about *L'Indifferent*. In disapproving of the museum's lax treatment of the painting, the press demonstrated feelings similar to those expressed by the thief.

A related situation is created when a public shares a thief's beliefs in cases such as theft for political reasons. In an unusual case in 2001, a man in Boulder, Colorado admitted to stealing 21 ceramic penises hanging from a clothesline as part of an exhibition on domestic violence in the town library. The theft gave fuel to an already brewing controversy as he left a flag in the phalluses' place. Some weeks before, after the attack on the World Trade Center,

---

[62] Esterow, 15.
[63] Ibid.
[64] Ibid., 206.

the library had rejected requests to hang a flag in the entrance of its building on the grounds that it might make some patrons uncomfortable. Arguments ensued, and after the theft, debates began concerning which item was more appropriate for display in a public library. Proclaiming himself "El Dildo Bandit," Bob Rowan called into a local radio show to confess to stealing the piece, saying that he felt the sculpture to be pornographic and the flag to be more appropriate for a public institution.[65] He returned the sculpture unharmed, and the library did not reinstall the work. For returning the work, Rowan was charged not with theft, but with public tampering and had to pay a small fine. In this case, the thief had taken the work because he did not enjoy the piece and saw its display using public resources as inappropriate, similar to the case of Bunton and the Goya. A little more than a week later, a second piece was stolen from the Boulder Public Library. This is widely seen as a copycat thief and illustrates the point that theft can lead to more thefts, particularly if punishments are lenient.

---

[65] Pam Regensberg, "Art Thief Rejects Plea Offer," *Daily Camera,* January 29, 2002.

Those Who Keep

Thus far, we have mostly examined cases in which the work was stolen by a party that did not desire to keep the work. The disparity in the examples discussed demonstrates the varied scope of art theft in the twentieth century. In each case, the culprits have a variety of motives for making use of a group's value for art. In other words, the thief steals the work because it is of value and by stealing it, he can satisfy his desires. The man who robbed the Boulder Library in 2001 wanted to bring attention to the library's refusal to hang an American flag, and was able to do so because of the value of art. The sculpture itself was not a well known work or one of great expense, but the idea of stealing any art is striking to the public because art seems sacred. It is worshipped in buildings meant to glorify it in hushed awe. For this reason, the public is fascinated by art theft and it receives wide media coverage. This "popularity" may be another reason some thieves are drawn to art theft; though they may not be able to tell their tale without being arrested, some thieves may seek to be a part of the glamour. This may also contribute to why some thieves, like Rowan and Bunton, decide to confess: for attention and public association with a sensational theft. Perhaps both wanted their names attached to the statement they made about displays using public resources.

For Friedrich Nietzsche, possession of an object does not mean literal ownership, but merely the ability to use the object.[66] If someone is able to observe a sculpture in a museum and be affected by it, then it could be said he possesses it. In this way, multiple people can possess a single work. If the work is stolen, the work is subsequently stolen from all of them, who are unable to have access to the work. Similarly, a museum's decision to place a work in storage may also be seen as robbing the public of its use. Nietzsche describes a second type of possession that may be applicable here. For some, using an object is not enough to feel a sense of possession, and so the possessor may desire more intimacy by having exclusive use of the object.[67] The possessor has control over the object, denying it to others, and thus has influence over others. He wants the good that others have all for himself, perhaps a result of being envious of others who have objects which he does not. Werner Muensterberger describes a similar personality type "that is driven by the need to own and to be in control, and simply unable to wait or to tolerate frustration."[68] This type of person places his own desires before the desires, and laws, of others, living according to his own "moral and psychological codes."[69]

This has widespread ramifications for Nietzsche, who describes art as the "will to life," making the unbearable daily grind more bearable.[70] If we think of art theft as the theft of a tool to help make life more bearable from those who use art, then there is potentially serious power imbedded in art theft. This power, though it may not be consciously recognized, may be felt by the thief and be a motivating factor. And there is another implication, for the thief does not simply take the work from those who use it contemporaneously, but also from those who might use it in the future. This thought is echoed in the words of Anna

---

[66] Friedrich Nietzsche, *Beyond Good and Evil,* trans. Walter Kaufmann (New York: Random House, 1989), paragraph 194.
[67] Ibid.
[68] Werner Muensterberger, *Collecting: An Unruly Passion* (Princeton, NJ: Princeton University Press, 1994), 228.
[69] Ibid.
[70] Friedrich Nietzsche, *Twilight of the Idols,* trans. R. J. Hollingdale (New York: Penguin Books, 1990), 4.

Kisluk, director of the Art Loss Register, an organization designed to curb art theft, "This is a loss not just to the art community, but to people everywhere who have lost the chance to see these wonderful works."[71] The thief potentially denies future generations access to the work and the ability to utilize the work, shaping in a small way the path that mankind takes as he may never again have access to the work or be influenced or guided by it. The thief controls not just individuals, but history, censoring what it may include, and affecting those who learn from this history.

This is not to say that all thieves are motivated by power. Thieves can also be motivated by a "mixture of love for art, awe at its financial value, and resentment that often comes from thwarted efforts to experience art in an intimate context."[72] In 1981, a security supervisor in a Baltimore Museum confessed to taking 81 pieces from the museum over a period of six weeks. He explained that he liked to touch the objects, but when the museum's conservation department added locks to its doors, handling the pieces became impossible, so he had to take the objects so that he could hold them.[73] The thief was denied what gave him pleasure, producing a feeling of frustration and an act of aggression against the museum that denied him access to what gave him pleasure. He was then able to satisfy his desires by holding the objects and creating what he felt was a satisfying relationship with the objects.

At the core of this case was a personal need for a relationship with the objects stemming from some event in the thief's psychological history that made him need the relationship. As Muensterberger writes, behind many longings for possessions, there is "often a memory of an early traumata or disillusionment, which then shifted the need for people to a narcissistic need for substitution functioning as their equivalent- in other words, a self-indulgence with objects."[74] People have proven to be an unreliable source of friendship, so a collector diverts his affections

---

[71] Brian MacQuarrie, "Priceless Loss Not Hopeless," *Boston Globe,* June 19, 1996.
[72] Burnham, 71.
[73] Conklin, 131.
[74] Muensterberger, 299.

into objects. Many connoisseur thieves justify their actions by saying, like Bogousslavsky, that institutions treat objects indifferently, or neglect objects, making it hard for others to appreciate them. When taken, the objects may not be missed and will be cherished by the person who takes them.[75] This person may associate the object with certain ideas, investing himself in the work, which produces an identification with the work and an intimate relationship.

The need for an individual to steal a work for himself puts a wrinkle in the ideas on which public collections are founded; if a public collection is a collection to be preserved for and used by the public, why do some feel they need to take the work for themselves? Perhaps they feel entitled to it more than others. Perhaps viewing the work is not enough, and someone wants to live with it and develop a more intimate relation with the work, as discussed above. In 1953, a 13-inch Rodin bronze *Psyche* was found in the Victoria and Albert Museum that had been taken from a London dealer four months prior. Under the sculpture was a note that read:

> There was no mercenary intent behind my abduction of this exquisite creature. I merely wished to live with her for a while. Auguste Rodin would have understood. The enclosed [$1.40] toward *Le Baiser* [another Rodin work for whose purchase the Tate Gallery was raising a public subscription] is all I can afford. An Impecunious Art Student.[76]

Here, the thief seems to have taken the work because the original setting in which he viewed the work did not allow for a personal enough relationship with the work. It is difficult to say whether the theft could have been prevented by the piece being displayed differently, unless perhaps the piece was not displaced at all, but kept secure from everyone.

Since objects stolen for someone's possession usually are not put up for sale, their recovery is difficult if they are not returned by the culprit, particularly if the victim does

---

[75] Conklin, 131
[76] Esterow, 21.

not realize the work has been taken. The Cooper-Hewitt Museum discovered it had lost a Rembrandt etching of *St. Jerome Reading* in 1972 when a scholar noticed that the picture had been replaced by an illustration of the etching taken from an exhibition catalog. Though they could not tell when the piece was taken, the FBI believed the etching to be permanently lost as the work was taken by a clever criminal. [77] The work was later returned to the museum by mail. In 1964, a painting by Giorgio Morandi was discovered to be have been stolen from the Pitti Palace in Florence, and left in its place was a copy of the original stuck to the frame with cellotape. On the back was written, "Thank you very much. I love Morandi. 18.3.64." [78] The date indicated that the copy had hung in public view for six weeks without notice, and the copy was only revealed when the tape holding the copy in place wore out and allowed it to fall to the floor. The museum officials vehemently argued that the thief had misdated the copy to throw the police off his trail, for if the copy had hung without notice, it might challenge the importance of the distinction between an original and a copy.

A similar case is connected to the theft of the *Mona Lisa* in 1911. Gery Pieret was a friend of the poet Guillaume Apollinaire, who used Pieret as a character in a series of short stories. Through Apollinaire, Pieret befriended Pablo Picasso, who bought a number of small Phoenician statuettes Pieret had stolen from the Louvre. [79] During the outcry against the Louvre over the theft of the *Mona Lisa*, Pieret sold another stolen statuette to the *Paris-Journal* which was campaigning against gross neglect in state museums. The Louvre first learned of the thefts when the newspaper ran the story of how Pieret had taken two statuettes in 1907 and sold them to a Parisian painter friend. Pieret did not reveal that the friend was Picasso, who knew the pieces had been stolen from the Louvre and used them as inspiration for his early cubist works, including *Les Demoiselles d'Avignon*. [80] If one compares the

---

[77] Burnham, 49.
[78] Middlemas, 91.
[79] Seymour Reit, *The Day They Stole the Mona Lisa* (New York: Summit Books, 1981), 63.
[80] McLeave, 21, and Esterow 150.

painting with photographs of the Iberian heads in Picasso's possession, one can see similarities to these particular statues, especially in the ears of the two central figures of the painting.

The incident is important as an example of how a major museum may have works taken from it without the institution realizing it; the Louvre had not noticed the missing pieces until the newspaper printed its story. Incidents such as these fuel the belief that institutions neglect works in their collections, as the *Paris-Journal* reported. Newspapers sometimes play strange roles in art theft cases, buying stolen works to write a story about the atrocities of art theft, while encouraging theft by giving it more attention and actually purchasing stolen works. The incident also demonstrates how intertwined the black market is with legitimate art practices. Not only do legitimate dealers sometimes act with questionable morals by dealing in works with questionable provenances, but here Picasso, one of the most renown names in art, is using stolen works as fodder to create legitimate works to sell. Perhaps Picasso would have painted *Les Demoiselles d'Avignon* in the same way without possessing the two stolen statuettes. But his having a close relationship with and being able to handle the pieces with them in his possession, as well as his fear of being caught with them, is likely to have changed the way that he thought about such works.

Those involved with art theft are not always easily distinguishable as villains. This is often the case when dealers do not check the provenance of works they buy because they know that the deal is too good to be true. Though they may not have been the actual ones stealing the works, they encourage theft through supporting it financially and could potentially be convicted as accessories. They seem to support a practice that would be detrimental to them, as there is little to prevent the thief from stealing the piece back from the dealer. However, knowing people who can get you what you desire is important for an art dealer if a client is looking for something specific. This will be discussed in more depth later.

Dealers are not the only partakers in the art theft game with a respectable facade. Museums also will reap the spoils of theft and overlook certain ethics. In 1988, the J.

Paul Getty Museum was accused of being irresponsible by the Italian government when it returned to an unnamed collector some pieces of ancient Greek sculpture that the Italian government believed were smuggled illegally from Sicily.[81] Instead of helping officials to determine whether the suspicions were valid, the Getty chose to protect the collector's identity and conceal the collector's source of the antiquities. Such a precedent encourages other questionable sources to conduct illicit acts, knowing that there are powerful institutions that will safeguard them. Similarly, buyers of stolen works may protect dealers who sell to them due to an idealization of the supplier who they feel has singled them out like a special child, giving them the first opportunity to buy certain objects.[82] In the case of the Getty, immoral collectors are able to use the museum to give their works a better reputation, and the institution is able to display a wider range of works, giving it a more prestigious appearance. The museum may also not want to offend any potential donors or financial investors, and there may even be a sense of fear of what the questionable character might do if the institution did not cooperate sufficiently. The institution may wish to avoid as much bad publicity as possible and handle the matter as quickly and quietly as possible, minimizing their participation in any resulting scandal.

The Boston Museum of Fine Arts was subject to several scandals during its 1970 anniversary exhibition. The first was the discovery that the museum had paid half a million dollars for 219 pieces of a Turkish treasure trove that had been looted from a burial site. Refusing to repatriate the pieces to Turkey, museum officials argued that they were doing the world a favor by keeping such a collection intact rather than let the pieces be scattered about the black market.[83] The museum's reasoning obscures the fact that the pieces were bought on the black market by the museum.

The second scandal was the accusation from Italy's foremost recoverer of stolen art, Rodolfo Siviero, that the museum had smuggled a Raphael painting out of Italy.

[81] Ibid., 193.
[82] Muensterberger, 238.
[83] McLeave, 214.

The museum said the painting came from an elderly private collector who was aging and wished his favorite painting to be enjoyed by the public, for the price of $600,000.[84] But Siviero traced the painting's pedigree to a convicted Italian art smuggler who sold the painting directly to the museum under the supervision of the museum's director, Perry Rathbone. The chief curator Hanns Swarzenski had carried the picture from Genoa to Boston, without attempting to obtain an Italian export license and without declaring it when leaving Italy or arriving in Boston. In 1971, the painting was returned to Italy on the provisions that charges against museum officials be dropped. The case is usually classified as a case of smuggling, as the work was paid for each time it changed hands. I include it here as an example of the countless like it that result in the theft of the patrimony of the work's country of origin. It is a theft from the citizens of Italy who would not be able to enjoy the piece. Due to its changing hands on the black market for years in order to find a buyer outside of Italy, the work was unknown to the public until it arrived in Boston. And to what purpose? So that the Boston Museum might have a centerpiece for its anniversary celebration. So that the people of Boston could boast the possession of a Raphael. And so that the director and chief curator could further their reputations as capable finders of impossible to locate old masterpieces.

As should be apparent, the high value placed on art and combined with lenient sentencing and a high probability of avoiding capture, as well as numerous other factors, creates a situation that is ripe for theft. The next section will delve deeper into the consequences of art theft, exploring how the art theft community impresses itself upon different groups of people as well as the art objects themselves.

---

[84] Ibid.

Repercussions

In discussing those involved in the stealing of a work of art, there was one large category missing. It is the category of people who are affected by the theft of an artwork, which can be broken down into a number of subcategories. These are the owner or institution from which a work is stolen, the insurers of a work if it is insured, the recovery teams if they are employed, the audience of the work, the greater public that hears about the work, the scholars or historians who study or would study the work, the artist of the work, the work of art itself, and those who deal with the stolen work. This list is, of course, not all-inclusive, and many people will fit into several categories at once. For this reason, the categories are less a means of classifying those involved as they are a way of classifying the effects a theft can have.

Some of these categories appear rather straightforward. The recovery squads of stolen art are affected by art theft in that it creates a need for their existence. Many police departments, such as those of Los Angeles and New York, have used public funds to create "art squads" to check the rise of art related crimes. There have also been several international organizations created, such as the Art Loss Register and a division of Interpol. The insurance company has to compensate the owner and is affected primarily monetarily. The company will often try to cut its losses by utilizing a loss adjuster to find the work for a fee. One way of doing so is to offer a reward, the payment of the reward being less than the painting's insured worth, so the insurance company decreases its losses. The insurance company has a vested interest in the recovery of the work, often leading to a discrepancy between it and the art squad's position on apprehending the culprits. When faced with the choice of recovering the work or the thief, the insurers invariable choose the work while the police choose the thief. Monetary investment forces the insurers to focus on the short term while police will be more concerned with preventing future crimes.

Scholars are affected primarily not by the recovery procedures, but by the actual absence of the work itself. A missing work of art can change the scholarship of an artist because the work could be eventually forgotten. Art theft removes evidence used to prove or disprove ideas about an artist and an artist's culture, distorting information and shaping history, if in a minor way. This is especially true if the work has not been photographed or otherwise documented in a detailed fashion. In contrast, the recovery of a work of art that has been long forgotten can change scholarship, which has to account for new ideas. Another repercussion of theft is that as the number of works with questionable provenances increases, the less sure scholars can be about their historical information. To use the example of the Boston Museum's Raphael, the history of the work had been fabricated for the media so that museum officials avoided suspicion. This means that if the fabrication had gone undetected, historians would not have been able to know where the work was at a certain point in time, and whether it had influenced artists in its vicinity. Diane De Grazia, the Cleveland Museum of Art's chief curator, has said that the hint of such fabrications "makes you question everything. You may have built up a reputation for years, and it comes tumbling down in one slap."[85] The scope of this problem becomes apparent when we remember that one in twenty paintings have questionable provenances and have been given new papers. Every year, tens of millions of museum visitors walk through the entrance of the

---

[85] Peter Landesman, "A Crisis of Fakes," *New York Times Magazine*, March 18, 2001, 52.

Getty, or the Boston Museum of Fine Arts, and never consider that they may have to evaluate for themselves the authenticity of what is being presented to them. A museum's presentation creates an institutional authority that is constructed to seem impregnable.[86] It should be clarified here that while I have only discussed a few cases of a museum's involvement in thefts, the Getty and the Boston Museum of Fine Arts should not be singled out. The pervasiveness of art theft means that any museum with a substantial art collection has probably bought stolen works, or been a subject of a theft, or in some other way been affected by theft, despite their impregnable appearance. As one dealer said, "I don't know how anyone in this business for a number of years could not have experienced art theft."[87]

Art theft's also affects artists' career and how the world views artists. If all of the works by an artist were stolen, then the artist could not be studied adequately and he would soon fade from the public's mind. The artist's reputation would suffer, usually because people want his work bad enough for it to be stolen. Conversely, the recovery of a work of art can lead to the rediscovery of an artist, boost an artist's reputation, and boost the value of an artist's work. But it is difficult to say how a theft affects other similar works of art. Prices on the open market may increase as the supply of works has diminished, but this danger may turn potential buyers away from such works.

The stolen work of art itself may go through various changes as well. Often works that are taken for ransom are stored in poor conditions, so the physical state of the work deteriorates. The work's appearance may also be altered to aid in its being smuggled out of a country, and these alterations can damage the work and its financial value on the open market, while raising its black market value as it is less easily traced. Many times paintings are cut from their stretchers and rolled, rather than the thieves taking the more cumbersome stretched painting. An example is Rembrandt's *Storm on the Sea of Galilee*, stolen during the 1990 theft from the Isabella Stewart Gardner Museum. The painting "was cut from its frame and the canvas rolled up. Paint chips were found on the gallery floor, and every-

---

[86] Ibid., 40.
[87] Ho, 167.

one agrees that the masterpiece has suffered."[88] Frames may also be discarded and unless the paperwork is stolen with the work, which it sometimes is, the pedigree of the work can be lost or at the least blurred. After the recovery of a work, it may bear certain scars that it contracted during its adventure, which if its owner chose, could act as witness to another chapter in the work's life. But most owners, especially institutions, will decide to have the work restored, if they are able, so that there is no mark to taint the object and the adventure can be forgotten.

The theft of a sensational work will also bring publicity and create a great stir. When the *Mona Lisa* was stolen in 1911 from the Louvre, it was discussed for weeks in the newspapers around the world. The talk increased people's familiarity with the work, as well as encouraged the public to be sympathetic to the lost work. Similarly, the sensational theft of a lesser known work will bring the same pubic attention to it, and the artist, increasing the renown of both. The Boulder Library theft is an example, for even though the stolen work on domestic violence was not well known, the theft brought the piece a great amount of publicity and spurred debates about the work's situation both locally and nationally.

A strange twist is the phenomenon of art theft as performance art. In San Francisco in 1995, two guerilla style artists stole several Picassos from the newly opened Modern Art Museum. During the theft, a statue by Jeff Koons was knocked over by accident. Police were baffled when the paintings were returned unharmed along with a videotape of the robbery. The two thieves dressed as "Andy Warhol" and "Vincent Van Gogh" included on the tape documentation of the planning of the heist and the actual heist itself. When arrested the two said they wanted exposure and were frustrated that the museum refused to show local artists while it received local arts funding. [89] They viewed their theft as politically motivated and a performance as the works were returned. While the theft was a product of the political situation in which the artists found themselves, the actions that they chose were influenced by the popularity of art theft in recent years, especially among

---

[88] MacQuarrie.
[89] *15 Minutes* (False Gods Productions, 1997).

the media. The artists wanted to perform an act against the museum, one that was aggressive but at the same time one that would gain them and their cause publicity. When asked why they turned themselves in, they replied, "We wanted the exposure."[90] They sought to capitalize on the value society places on art by using it as a tool to gain recognition.

The media attention of a theft can increase the audience for a work of art. After the theft of the *Mona Lisa*, record crowds flooded the Louvre not to see the painting, but to see the empty place where the work had been. Perhaps the empty place reflected an emptiness in the crowd, a felt void that needed to be filled. When the work was recovered in Italy, it was shown there for a short time before returning to France. The crowds for the exhibition were so large that "the Uffizi had had to remove many busts and statues to prevent them from being overturned and broken in the struggle to get near the painting."[91] While the *Mona Lisa* had been popular before, the increase in crowds demonstrates that the theft caused more people to become curious about the work of art and how a work of art could produce such a fuss. However, the events of World War I would soon overshadow the painting's adventure and the story has been widely forgotten. Nevertheless, the regular audience of the work expanded because of the theft to include more of the general public.

The1990 theft from the Isabella Stewart Gardner Museum of twelve paintings received tremendous attention, and, at a total estimated value of $300 million, has been called the largest art theft in United States history.[92] Immediately after the theft, the museum employed a media relations organization, Wanger Associates, to handle the overwhelming international media attention.[93] According

[90] Ibid.

[91] Esterow, 170.

[92] Federal Bureau of Investigations, 2002, *Theft Notices: The Isabella Stewart Gardner Museum*, 2001 ed., Available [Online]: <http://www.fbi.gov/hq/cid/arttheft/isabella/isabella.htm> [April 20, 2002].

[93] Wanger Associates, 2002, *Robbery at the Isabella Stewart Gardner Museum*, 2001 ed. Available [Online]: <http://www.wangerassociates.com/Case_Studies/Robbery_at_the_Isabella_Stewart_Gardner_Museum.htm> [April 20, 2002].

to Wanger Associates, the theft had both positive and negative consequences. Assurances had to be offered to the public, trustees, major donors, museum members and staff "that the theft was an isolated incident and that the loss of a number of important paintings would not, in the long run, seriously diminish the appeal or the importance of the collection.[94] A story had to be generated "that attributed the cause of the theft to human error without making scapegoats out of the guards," and that maintained that the museum's security system "was state of the art."[95] It was continually stated that "there was no drop off in attendance, after the museum reopened;" instead, there was a rise in attendance immediately following the theft.[96] Because the paintings were highly renown and their loss could not be concealed, as much media coverage as possible was supported "in order to increase the chances of someone spotting the stolen paintings."[97] This increased press coverage offered an avenue through which the museum could encourage the media "to write about the Gardner's extraordinary architecture" and " about the museum's outreach programs."[98] Subsequent stories included a feature story in the *Smithsonian* magazine.[99] The museum was able to take its incident of art theft and use it to increase its publicity and spread knowledge about a number of its more positive attributes. However, the museum has also been criticized for "the unprofessional guard behavior of two young art school students who had been trained for only a week."[100] The increased positive and negative press that resulted from the theft increased the public's awareness of the museum and altered its ideas of the museum, demonstrating how the art theft community can affect art world institutions' images and audiences.

The audience that sees a work, aside from the owner, has a relation with the work of art that does not usually involve financial investment. Instead, its investment is solely

---

[94] Ibid.
[95] Ibid.
[96] Ibid.
[97] Ibid.
[98] Ibid.
[99] Ibid.
[100] Conklin, 126.

in the work's ability to function in an aesthetic capacity, and through the use of the work in this endeavor, the audience may begin to feel an attachment with the work, a possession, without paying for the work as owners. Why a work of art appeals to someone is a very complex and individual matter, but can involve identifying with the viewer's idea of the artist, making the art an intimate communication of an idea between the two. Or a viewer can associate a work of art with another object which the viewer desires and he may project his desire into the work of art. The loss of this object can be very traumatic depending on the strength of the viewer's connection with the object. As the viewer is investing himself into the work, when it is stolen, it is as if a part of him is stolen, there being no object in which to reflect or externalize himself. The usual suddenness of an art theft does not allow the audience to be weaned off the object to which they have become attached. There is no warning until the sudden realization that the object is gone, which may result in depression and a need for reparation.

The work of art is a tool for the audience with which to handle their identity and reality, and their identity and reality are disturbed by the theft of this tool. Often art will serve as an object that, through the projection of the self into the work to be observed by the viewer as a whole, satisfies a need to attach the self to an object. The object can be used to ward off a deep sense of anguish and the pride in possessing the object can enhance or restore a narcissistically injured person's sense of self.[101] By demonstrating his attachment to and knowledge about the object to others, the possessor (one who feels they possess the work as different from the owner who has bought the work) elicits acclaim from those around him. This makes him feel special and worthy of the object. When a work of art is taken, so is this sense of security and worth, which can be replaced with a sense of chaos, a threat of death, distrust, fear, and many other responses depending upon the nature of one's relation to the work.

The owner of the artwork may or may not be affected in this way, but is in addition touched by the loss of a financial investment. Even if a work is insured, a private

---

[101] Muensterberger, 235.

owner may lose a significant amount of money when a work is stolen because many works are underinsured to keep premiums low. This financial loss will intensify other feelings of loss felt by the owner. In such cases, an owner may seek to blame other parties, such as the police or an employed security service. Such was the case when the Nathan Silberberg Galleries suffered a loss of approximately $2 million in art work and afterward sued its security service for this amount, though its contract specifically stated that the security service was only liable for $250.[102]

A museum or other institution may have a larger collection and so an individual theft is not as great, or as personal, a loss in proportion. However, it can be just as damaging. Anne Hawley, the Gardner Museum director, has said the museum's 1990 loss is "like a death in the family."[103] Joan Norris, the museum's marketing director, has made a similar remark: "it's like we are gathered for a holiday and some of our family members are missing."[104] Victim's fears that accusations of carelessness in security and other bad publicity will influence investors that they should not associate their name, or their funds, with the institution is evident in the Gardner's reassurances after its theft. Publicity of an art theft may also reveal weak points in security and might lead to more thefts. For matters of saving face and of finance, many museums and some collectors do not report thefts. Police record only 50% to 60% of all art thefts, and Interpol, an international organization that supports authorities whose mission is preventing or detecting international crime, is notified less than 10% of the time.[105]

The last category of those who are touched by art theft are those who actually deal in stolen art. Unlike most of the other categories, these individuals chose to be affected by planning their participation in the theft. For this reason, many of the repercussions they feel for taking a work are connected to their motives for doing the act. Other effects, like those of guilt, secrecy, fear of being

---

[102] Nathan Silberberg Galleries v. Holmes Protection, 618 NYS 2d 3 NY Ct. of Appeals 1994.

[103] MacQuarrie.

[104] Ibid.

[105] Middlemas, 76.

caught or turned in, being caught, and serving a sentence, are not chosen by the lawbreaker, but can be weighed against the benefits of theft and seen as acceptable. There is also the possibility that a thief may actually desire to be caught for various reasons. Perhaps the criminal already has feelings of guilt and so wishes to perform an act for which he would be punished. Or perhaps he has been called a delinquent so many times that he is convinced he is one and so has to do something to confirm that he is a delinquent. Such psychological reasons for committing a crime shape the thief's response to the consequences of a theft, whether they be jail time or not being caught at all. For them it is a way of acting out what they already believe to be a reality.

Thieves also steal in order to capitalize on society's value of art. But they do not just feed off this value; by influencing the value, thieves influence the market and all those who are connected with that market, causing an interaction between the art theft community and the legitimate art world. In the next section, I will relate several interviews I have conducted to demonstrate how specific dealers who work in the art market are touched by the art theft community.

Interviews

The Chiaroscuro Market

.

Up to this point, this paper has been largely conceptual. Drawing from the available literature, I have examined cases and their analysis to develop theories for understanding the art theft community and how it operates. To reiterate, it is my argument that this community is not only attached to the legitimate art world, but is in fact intertwined with it to such a degree that the two affect each other in substantial ways. There are a variety of motivations for those who participate in art theft, but many of these motivations, including that of monetary gain, are fueled by the high value that is given to art in the legitimate art world. There are also a variety of repercussions from art theft that alter the way the public interacts with art and the way art is consumed by scholars, collectors, and institutions. These repercussions can be observed in the physical security measures taken to prevent theft, in the purchasing of insurance, and in subtle ways such as uncertainty over provenances. As it affects groups in the legitimate art world, art theft affects the value placed on works and influences how future thefts will occur.

The claim that there are two art worlds, a legitimate and a black market one, mutually affecting each other is a bold one. To corroborate this claim, I conducted a series of interviews with art dealers in New York. I chose dealers who trade in works by non-living artists because a work by a non-living artist is likely to have a pedigree for dealers to verify. My logic for doing so was to determine if galleries are confronted with certain repercussions of art theft as I have laid them out. These repercussions, as discussed in the last chapter, include alterations to the artwork itself, suspicious provenances, absences in scholarship, as well as an awareness of unlawful dealers around them.

My initial discussions were brief as I found most of those to whom I talked did not want to answer questions specifically concerning art theft. I found that in my interviews, most dealers felt more comfortable describing a market where reputable dealers are confronted with others who have bad reputations for being unconcerned with a work's authenticity or history of ownership. While some mentioned that there were dealers who were not ethical in their acquisition practices, only two of six brought up that there are dealers who seem unconcerned by dealing with stolen art. Many expressed a concern for a lack of regulations in the art world, but did not desire to have any additional legal responsibilities placed upon them that additional regulations might involve.

The first fruitful conversation I had was with Martha Fleischman from the Kennedy Galleries in New York, which deals mostly with work from the eighteenth, nineteenth, and twentieth centuries. Fleischman stated that often the work that she evaluates to be taken in by the gallery is "not well documented" and "these days you have to be suspicious."[106] She says that there are certainly dealers "who have bad reputations and who you don't want to work with."[107] However, she believes it is good policy to know all the players and talk to everyone, even if there are some you dismiss more readily than others, for the gallery has a kind of wish list, as well as a client wish list, that it hopes to fill. According to Fleischman, the gallery checks all of the provenances of pieces it takes in, but because of poor documentation and the length of some pieces' histories, one can never be certain about the history of ownership of works. She also stated that some have a reputation

---

[106] Martha Fleischman of the Kennedy Galleries, interview by author, New York, New York, April 18, 2002.
[107] Ibid.

for being less thorough than other galleries in their research of provenance. This suggests that some galleries are more diligent in verifying that they are not selling stolen work. While the gallery researches the provenances, it cannot be sure that what it sells has not at some time been falsified to disguise that it is stolen. Simultaneously, Fleischman recognizes that there are other dealers who are less concerned about researching a work to make sure it is legitimate.

Lisa Skrabek of the Babcock Galleries said many similar things. The Babcock Galleries, founded in 1852, specializes in works of the nineteenth and early twentieth centuries. Ideally, the gallery seeks work that has a solid provenance and which has not been altered in appearance, but this is "rarely found."[108] Skrabek describes most pieces the gallery evaluates for purchase or to be taken on consignment as poorly documented and with provenances that are not solid. Though provenances are researched, everyone at the Babcock Galleries is "an expert," and often works are judged "primarily by instinct."[109] While she is confident in the quality of work at the Babcock Galleries, she notes that works sold by the gallery are researched to the best of the staff's ability, but carry no warrantee. Skrabek does say that there are collections from which those in the art world who are above board do not buy. Here, the gallery would not intentionally distribute stolen works, but everyone makes mistakes. And once the work is sold, the gallery is not responsible if the work is later found to have oddities in its history, though to maintain their reputation, many galleries, including the Babcock Galleries, will buy back works in such circumstances. Such was the case when the Spanierman Gallery produced the Dow that Crawford had stolen.[110]

Morgan Spangel of the Beardston Gallery, which represents modern and contemporary pieces, went further. Though he knows the majority of people he dealt with, occasionally he is confronted with a work about which he

---

[108] Lisa Skrabek of the Babcock Galleries, interview by author, New York, New York, April 18, 2002.
[109] Ibid.
[110] Los Angeles Police Department.

knows "something is wrong."[111] This presents a problem as he might want something else in their collection, and so does not want to offend the seller by suggesting the seller is offering an illicit work. He cited a recent case he encountered in which he was offered a Franz Kline by someone he knew. However, he was suspicious of the work, and so he consulted an expert who also believed that "something was definitely wrong."[112] For this reason he did not purchase the work, but took no further action, such as notifying the seller why he refused the work or notifying any authorities. According to Spangel, it is not his responsibility to notify anyone, as it was only his opinion that the work was suspicious. For this reason, he says he does not worry that the piece will remain on the market for someone else to buy.[113]

To assure the integrity of these interviews, all of the dealers I conversed with were members of the Art Dealers Association of America (ADAA). This is mostly a prestige association, as membership is exclusive and not required in order to deal art in the United States. Initiate members have to be sponsored and voted in unanimously, voting being based on the reputation of the initiate, who must have a business history of more than five years. The ADAA has guidelines for its members, though those I talked to did not necessarily know these guidelines, one of which is "assisting the F.B.I. and other law enforcement agencies on issues involving stolen works of art, questions of authenticity and in identifying fake works and attempting to remove them from the market."[114]

Skrabek is one who, though a member of the ADAA, was not aware of any ADAA guidelines concerning questions of authenticity.[115] Another dealer of modern and contemporary art, who asked to remain nameless, said that the art market was full of gray areas and that dealers at his

---

[111] Morgan Spangel of the Beardston Galleries, interview by author, New York, New York, April 18, 2002.
[112] Ibid.
[113] Ibid.
[114] Art Dealers Association of America, 2002, *Who We Are: General Activities*, 2001 ed., Available [Online]: <http://www.artdealers.org> [April 19, 2002].
[115] Skrabek.

gallery did not necessarily scrutinize the history of a work. Steuart Osha at David Tunick, Inc. said that she was "not sure of any guidelines in the Art Dealer's Association," or of any guidelines of the American government concerning knowledge of the history of works.[116] Osha went on that there are certainly "people that no one wants to work with because there are lots of things you don't know about the history of their works."[117] Occasionally they are dealt with because "different clients have different criteria."[118] However, Osha was unaware of any insurance measure that could be taken out on a work in the case that it is not what it is purported to be besides checking the Art Loss Register, which is part of standard procedure.

Henry Allsopp of Dickinson Roundell, Inc., a gallery dealing with old master paintings, Impressionist, modern, post-war and contemporary art, said that he knew the ADAA had authenticating guidelines, but he had never read them.[119] Allsopp expressed that Dickinson Roundell, Inc. had several in-house experts in a variety of fields and to authenticate an unfamiliar work, these experts' primary method was to check the catalog raisonne of the pertinent artist. He also mentioned that it was routine to check the Art Loss Register's list of stolen works, though he suspected that other dealers do not do so out of routine. If a catalog raisonne is not available or a work is not in a catalog raisonne, then there can often be "a gray area," though the gallery may still buy the work.[120] He offered an example of a Modigliani the gallery had recently taken in that was not in the artist's catalog raisonne, but had a stamp demonstrating it had been handled by the gallery that deals with Modigliani's estate. While a number of experts had doubts abut the history of the work, the gallery felt comfortable taking on the work. Often times dealers are faced with shaky provenances and holes in scholarship, and are forced to make difficult evaluations.

---

[116] Steuart Osha of David Tunick, Inc., interview by author, New York, New York, April 18, 2002.
[117] Ibid.
[118] Ibid.
[119] Henry Allsopp of Dickinson Roundell, Inc., interview by author, New York, New York, April 18, 2002.
[120] Ibid.

Allsopp also noted that art dealing is "totally unregu-
lated ... there is no government or legal body to govern.
The law is gray; lawsuits swing both ways and there are no
real precedents," and "anyone can make mistakes."[121]He,
like Skrabek and Fleischman, acknowledged that there are
certain collections with suspicious reputations, and there
are also collections in which some of the works might be
exquisite while others were questionable. He cited as an
example a collection with which he has dealt that has
many good Impressionist works, but works by old masters
that are not well grounded.[122] Allsopp also went so far as to
say that there are "lots of people who you cannot trust ...
people who are known to be unscrupulous.... There is a
network of unscrupulous dealers and it is amazing to legitimate dealers that they stay afloat."[123] He continued that
"you see those who are dodgy and know who to avoid.
There are people that everyone knows are dodgy."[124] He
also expresses a concern that often new people in the business do not have the luxury of avoiding dealers with bad
reputations; dealing art is "a hard business to get into and
people will do anything to stay in business. There is not a
lot of big money, so you have to grab what you can."[125]

Allsopp's comments clearly indicate that he feels the
presence of numerous immoral dealers. Some may not
make substantial inquiries about the origins of works they
take in, as when the Spanierman Gallery took in the stolen
Dow. Others make take in and distribute works that they
explicitly know are illicit. Mahboubian sought to sell
works explicitly after he recognized faults in his collection.
These are the type of dealer that sells stolen works. Allsopp's need to be aware of these dealers in order to avoid
being duped is one way that dealers are touched by the art
theft community. A second way is having to compete with
such dealer for sales, as the less moral a dealer is in attain-
ing a work, the more works he can offer at low prices.

In 1998, Hector Feliciano, a journalist and author,
was interviewed by Robert Fishko, editor of the *ADAA*

---

[121] Ibid.
[122] Ibid.
[123] Ibid.
[124] Ibid.
[125] Ibid.

Report, on the topic of stolen art and the commerce of art. Representing the ADAA, Fishko stated that currently a stolen painting could be sold in Switzerland and then in America, and if no claims are made against the work, the owner has a legal title.[126] He continued that the fact that it was stolen "taints the painting from a moral and an ethical point of view, but from the point of view of commerce and legality, for me not to touch the painting, I feel, would require all dealers to unite and say they are not going to knowingly traffic in goods of this kind."[127] But he also recognizes that something stronger than an agreement between dealers is necessary, such as an international body of laws.

Art dealing is an international business and currently the laws between countries vary considerable. Where in France a dealer can be found guilty of misrepresenting a work or forging documents appearing to establish a work's authenticity, in England and America, laws are not so clear cut and lawsuits do not set a clear precedent.[128] Until there are internationally agreed upon laws, as Fishko says, "we are left with the individual art dealers. Art dealers who may well ask, why should they be in a position of substituting their ethics for the laws of commerce, why should they have to pay when they are not the guilty ones?"[129] Feliciano agrees, and adds that many dealers are afraid that such regulations will "create too many constraints on their daily lives, and on their jobs."[130] More regulations will only be useful if they are obeyed.

Many of the dealers that I talked to admitted openly that they did not know the current guidelines, such as those laid out by the ADAA, that they should follow. Spangel even described an interaction in which he violated these guidelines by not "assisting the F.B.I. and other law enforcement agencies on issues involving stolen works of

---

[126] Art Dealers Association of America, 2002, *ADAA Report*, 2002 ed., Available [Online]: <http://www.artdealers.org/news/looted.html> [April 24, 2002].
[127] Ibid.
[128] Russell Taylor and Brian Brooke, *The Art Dealers* (New York: Charles Scribner's Sons, 1996), 277.
[129] Art Dealers Association of America, *ADAA Report*.
[130] Ibid.

art, questions of authenticity and in identifying fake works and attempting to remove them from the market." If this is a representation of typical behavior, one can see how unscrupulous characters can take advantage of this behavior in deals that are built largely on trust. Stolen works can make their way onto the open market and be sold for a different price than if they were being sold by their legitimate owners. The values of legitimate works are disrupted when buyers compare them to works with similar qualities that are stolen. These buyers may not be aware, or care to be aware, that works they inspect are stolen. As Osha said, "different clients have different criteria." This is one way art theft causes the value of works of art to change. In the next section, I will look at how society values art and how theft is an important part of the construction of this value.

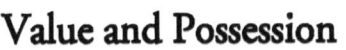

Value and Possession

The Chiaroscuro Market

Art is only stolen if it is valuable, with value coming in two connected forms, economic and cultural. A work that is culturally valuable is likely to have a high economic value, and an intense bidding war for a work may raise cultural interest in the work. Each community has a separate appreciation for works of art, and so a work will receive different prices and praises depending upon where it is located in the world. Inversely, each work of art is unique and so there is no way of creating a standard system to evaluate artworks. Instead, the value of a work of art is based on individuals' beliefs. The group of individuals who value a piece may be many sizes, but this does not affect the value of the piece for that group. The altarpiece of a small church may be just as priceless to its parish as the *Mona Lisa* is to its audience. While the economic value reflects the cultural and historical importance of a work to a group, it also includes the current fashion in art, perception of good investment, the promotional elements of the owner or dealer, the artist's reputation, the scarcity of similar works, the work's provenance, and its physical size, weight, and condition.[131] Through these variables, the value of a work of art is constructed in a collective effort.

---

[131] Conklin, 17.

For any work whose artist is known, the idea of the artist will shape the way that the work is assessed and the meaning that is assigned to it. But the artist creates with contributions from the manufacturers of materials, from other artists who help to develop an artistic tradition, from critics who assess work, and from galleries who exhibit and finance work. If a work's history is challenged, it disturbs the connections to all these sources. The Spanierman Gallery's reputation was affected by its involvement in the Dow theft. The widespread faking of the provenances of Dali prints has lowered the prices of Dali prints and drawings and marred the reputations of both the artist and the printers connected.[132] The acts have not only changed the value of the works which were involved, but also influenced what the public associates with the artist, with similar works by that artist, and with all involved. The artist's reputation, a collective activity of historians, critics, dealers, and artists, is shaken, sending ripples out towards those tied with the artist's work. In the end, an artist's reputation lasts because of a critical mass of work being available, an important clientele, and those who have an emotional or financial stake in keeping an artist's memory alive and linked to a school of artists, a region, or a community. All of these have an investment in the oeuvre of an artist, and when works of an artist disappear, it may be felt by each of them.

As consumers of art, collectors are an integral part of the creation of the value of art. A collection can be used as a form of expression for the collector and the seeking out of works can be an adventure, with collectors competing with one another. The collection may also become an obsession for the collector, who transfers all of his desires, and resources, into it. The collector preserves art and gains knowledge about his works, giving acquisition a noble purpose. The objects become sacred, and take on distinctions and personalities of their own. It is typical for collectors to personify favorite works; Freud is known to have

---

[132] Lee Canterall, 2002, *The Great Dali Art Fraud: An Update*, 2001 ed., Available [Online]: <http://www.pixi.com/~hicatt/abuses.htm> [April 21, 2002].

said "Good morning" to the Chinese statuettes he had collected and kept in his office.[133]

The collection becomes a way of presenting the self to the world and of measuring oneself, becoming a map of the self-image and what one wishes to be. This is accomplished in part by signifying events in the collector's personal history, reminding him of family history or the time in his life when the work was acquired. He can view the work, hold the work unimpeded, and through careful selection and arrangement, his collection becomes a gestalt.

Theft disrupts this gestalt, influencing not just the way the one piece is perceived, but how the whole is perceived. It disturbs the collection's ability to express the collector, and in looking at the self that is reflected in the broken collection, the collector feels something is missing; a part of him is gone. Theft may also affect the value of the collection as a whole, as the complete collection may have a greater financial value than the sum of its parts. For the adamant collector, a theft is perceived as a loss of part of the self, a part that is missing and may be in great danger.

Curators and museum directors often feel the same intimate connection with their collection as private collectors, as expressed by the Gardner Museum's staff, and though they do not invest their own personal finances in the works, they do invest their careers in acquisitions. Regular viewers may also feel similar feelings to what the collector feels. But institutions like museums aid in the construction of value in a different way because of the large amounts of viewers that access them. The reputation of a museum adds to the value of a work, as does restoration work and publicity, but unlike collectors, museums rarely deaccession a work of art. The work increases in cultural and financial value and desirability, but there is no way for anyone else to purchase the work. The inability to obtain the work along with the work's high desirability is a perfect receptacle for a collector's jealousy and a target for theft.

Art theft satisfies a need. It is a means to an end and that end embodies a value. Some needs are fundamental; one cannot survive without filling them. Others are felt

[133] Russell Belk, *Collecting in a Consumer Society* (New York: Routledge, 1995), 146.

needs that the one in need perceives as necessary, and the denial of the need may be detrimental to one's mental health due to the strength of one's beliefs.[134] The very word "need" implies that the one in need has a claim that has to be met. Over the course of history, needs take different forms in society, with certain wants that are merely desirable becoming felt needs that are psychologically necessary.

The nature of the need for art has been much debated and art has consequently been seen to fulfill several needs. Hegel believed art is necessary in order to realize one's self, similar to throwing a stone into a pond to visualize one's effect on the world.[135] Another perspective is to see the work of art as a therapeutic object to which one relates through the projection of the self into the object, which is returned when the object is internalized. Art can operate like a mirror that we trust to be there and to help see ourselves. Art can be used to empower oneself, and often those who need empowerment the most are those who cannot access art, and so must gain possession of it through illicit means. It is this sort of distress of reality that art is used to ease. Unsatisfied with one's access to a work in the art world that raises one spiritually, some perceive it necessary to possess a particular work through other means, essentially removing the work from this art world and involving it in a criminal world.

This is true of both those who take works for themselves and those who buy works that are stolen. In art theft, there are few completely innocent buyers, as each buyer is responsible for assuring himself of the authenticity of the work and title that he is purchasing.[136] Buyers believe it necessary to risk the consequences of possessing stolen art in order to fulfill a need, and even those who are ignorant of art theft's pervasiveness are guilty of not being a responsible buyer. The actions of the art theft community add to the responsibilities of all who trade in art and it is those who trade in art who feel the consequences

---

[134] Maureen Ramsey, *Human Needs and the Market* (Brookfield VM: Ashgate Publishing Company, 1992), 7,10.
[135] Ian Fraser, *Hegel and Marx: The Concept of Need* (Edinburgh: Edinburgh University Press, 1998), 102.
[136] Burnham, 49.

if these responsibilities are not seen to. Those who are not responsible buyers help to create an environment where art theft can flourish and works can be reintroduced into the market. To be clear, I do not intend to imply that all those who are uninformed and buy stolen works are necessarily criminals. Instead, I wish to demonstrate that some are more diligent than others about verifying that they are not purchasing stolen art. This variance creates a gray area between the black market and the open market, as seen in *Porter v. Wertz*. In this area it can become difficult to determine where the black market ends and the open market begins.

Conclusions

The Chiaroscuro Market

Ideally, art should be an integral part of one's life and should lend an aspect of art to one's life. It is my opinion that the consequences of art theft, smuggling, and the distribution of stolen works affect, to a degree, the perception of all works of art. Because of this, art theft affects all who have an interest in art in a profound way, though art theft's secretive nature often means that its consequences are obscured. It is in part due to art theft that art's value has become detrimental to itself; its value is so high that its functioning is hindered by security measures. In an ideal world, works would be available to all who wanted to view them, to use them to transfigure their thoughts and perceptions, but deterrents against theft often prohibit this. [137] Certainly many works are available for viewing through reproductions, but a reproduction does not contain the same aura as the original. Viewing a reproduction is a different act than interacting with the physical object of the original which one can hold, turnover in one's hands, and notice the details history has engraved on it. Art's value hindering its use might suggest that the balance between value and function has been upset, but art receives its value because someone wants to own it. Someone wants to possess it and have it perform a function for them. It is the theft of this

---

[137] Ibid., 241.

function that makes art theft traumatic, and the production of this trauma is one way in which the art theft community interacts with the legitimate art world. Art thefts come with other repercussions as well, and these repercussions stretch out into the art world, changing many of its aspects in slight, but significant, ways. At the same time, the art theft community is dependant upon the art world for a supply of art and regulations to circumvent. The two are in a relationship, each responding to the other.

The western art world is fortunate to have so many means through which it can curb art theft. These means include security measures, disseminating information about stolen works, ethical acquisition policies, auction and dealer regulations, statutes of limitation reforms, and recovery teams like art squads. But these measures do little to control a central component of art theft - the value of art. As long as we value art, it will continue to be stolen, and as it is unlikely that we will reach an apex in our valuing of art, theft will continue to grow despite the best efforts of law enforcement agencies and security techniques. This illustrates the intertwined nature of the art theft community and the legitimate art world. Art theft will always benefit some and cause trauma to others. Understanding the phenomenon of art theft and its relationship to the art world can help us to deal with it, not only in apprehending those involved in the art theft community, but also in dealing with the loss of works and other repercussions.

Further Reading

15 Minutes (False Gods Productions, 1997).

Laurie Adams, *Art Cop: Robert Volpe* (New York: Dodd, Mead, 1974).

Konstantin Akinsha, *Stolen Treasure: The Hunt for the World's Lost Masterpieces* (London: Weidenfeld and Nicolson,1995).

Konstantin Akinsha, "The Mafia Moves in Moscow," *Art News,* December 1990, 142-43.

"All is Not Lost," *Art Review,* v. 53, May 2001, 15.

"Art Smuggling," *Art Journal,* Spring 1972.

Martin Bailer, "Art Theft: No Respect for the Sacred," *Art Newspaper,* July/August 2001, 7.

Martin Bailer, "The Turkish Picassos," *Art Newspaper,* June 2001, 5.

J. Barelli, *On the Business of Art and Antique Theft,* Diss., Fordham University, 1986.

Paul Bator, *The International Trade in Art* (Chicago: University of Chicago Press, 1981).

Russell Belk, *Collecting in a Consumer Society* (New York: Routledge, 1995).

Neil Brodie, "The Property Market," *Museums Journal,* October 2000, 17.

Bonnie Burnham, *The Art Crisis* (New York: St. Martin's Press, 1975).

Bonnie Burnham, *Art Theft: Its Scope, Its Impact, and Its Control* (New York: International Foundation for Art Research, Inc., 1978).

Bonnie Burnham, "The Black Market in Art," *Art News*, January 1976, 80.

Ronald Burns, " Culture as a Determinant of Crime: An Alternative Perspective," *Environment and Behavior*, May 2000, 347-360.

James Clifford, "On Collecting Art and Culture," *The Visual Culture Reader*, ed. Nick Mirzoeff (London: Routledge, 1999).

John Conklin, *Art Crime* (London: Praeger, 1994).

Convention on the Means of Prohibiting and Preventing the Illicit Import, Export, and Transfer of Ownership of Cultural Property, UNESCO, 1970.

The Cultures of Collecting, ed. John Elsner and Roger Cardinal (Cambridge ,MA: Harvard University Press, 1994).

Leonard D. DuBoff, *Art Law in a Nutshell* (St Paul, Minnesota: West Publishing Company, 1993).

Milton Esterow, *Art Stealers* (New York: Macmillan, 1973).

Ian Fraser, *Hegel and Marx: The Concept of Need* (Edinburgh: Edinburgh University Press, 1998),

Lisa Guersney, "Is Theft in the Eye of the Beholder," *New York Times*, September 6, 2001, G1.

Truc-Nhu Thi Ho, *Art Theft in New York City: An Exploratory Study in Crime Specificity*, Diss., Rutgers University, 1992.

Truc-Nhu Thi Ho, "Prevention of Art Theft at Commercial Art Galleries," *Studies on Crime and Crime Prevention,* v. 7, no. 2, 1998, 213-219.

Interpreting Objects and Collections, ed. Susan M. Pearce (New York: Routledge, 1994).

Harmer Johnson, *Guide to the Arts of the Americas* (New York: Rizzoli, 1992).

Joshua Kaufman, "Fake Forgeries and Stolen Art: Who Pays the Piper," *Art Business News*, October 2001, 108.

Judith Russi Kirchner, "Thieves Like Us," *Artforum*, September 1982, 40-42.

Peter Landesman, "A Crisis of Fakes," *New York Times Magazine*, March 18, 2001.

Law, Ethics, and the Visual Arts, ed. John H. Merryman and Albert E. Elsen (Philadelphia, PA: University of Philadelphia Press, 1987).

Donald Mason, *The Fine Art of Art Security* (New York: Van Nostrand Reinhold Co., 1979).

Hugh McLeave, *Rogues in the Gallery: The Modern Plague of Art Thefts* (Boston: D. R. Godine, 1981).

Souren Melikian, "Above Suspicion," *Art and Auction*, v. 23, no. 6, (2001), 44-50.

The Metropolitan Museum of Art, Art Theft Seminar for FBI Agents, May 1983.

The Metropolitan Museum of Art, Museum Security and Art Theft Conference, May 1983.

The Metropolitan Museum of Art, Museum Security and Art Theft Conference, January 1982.

Karl Meyer, *The Plundered Past* (New York Atheneum, 1973).

Robert Middlemas, *The Double Market: Art Theft and Art Thieves* (Farnborough: Saxon House, 1975).

Elizabeth Minchelli, "Black Market Art," *Art and Antiques*, Summer 2000, 130-132.

E. Moat, *Memoirs of an Art Thief* (London: Arlington Books, 1976).

Jane Morris, "Stealing Beauty," *Museums Journal*, April 2000, 20-23.

Werner Muensterberger, *Collecting: An Unruly Passion* (Princeton, NJ: Princeton University Press, 1994).

Museum Association Security Committee, Washington, DC, Art Theft Seminar, "FBI Stolen and Recovered Art File," June 1984.

Lynn H. Nicholas, *The Rape of Europa* (New York: Alfred A. Knopf, 1994).

Friedrich Nietzsche, *Beyond Good and Evil,* trans. Walter Kaufmann (New York: Random House, 1989).

Friedrich Nietzsche, *Twilight of the Idols,* trans. R. J. Hollingdale (New York: Penguin Books, 1990).

Patrick J. O'Keefe, *Trade in Antiquities: Reducing Destruction and Theft* (London: Archetype, 1997).

Susan M. Pearce, *Collecting in Contemporary Practice* (London: Sage Publications, 1998).

Maureen Ramsey, *Human Needs and the Market* (Brookfield VM: Ashgate Publishing Company, 1992).

David Ramus, *Gravity of Shadows*(New York: Harper Collins Publishers, 1998).

David Ramus, *Thief of Light* (New York: Harper Collins Publishers, 1995).

Recovery of Stolen Art: A Collection of Essays, ed. Norman Palmer (London: Kluwer Law International, 1998).

Pam Regensberg, "Art Thief Rejects Plea Offer," *Daily Camera,* January 29, 2002.

Reid Christine, "More Art Stolen From the Library," *Daily Camera*, November 20, 2001.

Recommendation for the Protection of Movable Cultural Property, UNESCO, 1978.

Seymour Reit, *The Day They Stole the Mona Lisa*(New York: Summit Books, 1981).

Jurgen Schick, *The Gods are Leaving the Country: Art Theft From Nepal* (Bangkok: White Orchid Press, 1998).

William Spain, "Art Crimes of the Century," *Art and Antiques*, Summer 2000, 98-103.

Robert Spiel, *Art Theft and Forgery Investigation: The Complete Field Manual* (New
York: Charles C. Thomas Publishers Ltd., 2000).

Susan Stewart, *On Longing* (Baltimore: The Johns Hopkins University Press, 1984).

Robin Thomas, *Protecting Cultural Objects in the Global Information Society: The Making of Object ID* (New York: Getty Information Institute, 1997).

Unidroit Convention on Stolen or Illegally Exported Cultural Objects, Rome, June 24, 1995.

Art Theft Conference , University of Delaware, 1978.

John Varoli, "Purloined Harem Girls, and Other Russian Mysteries," *New York Times*, November 28, 2001, E2.

Carol Vogel, "Experts Says Topeka Postal Item Is Stolen Chagall," *New York Times*, February 15, 2002.

Peter Watson, *Caravaggio Conspiracy* (Garden City: Double Day, 1984).

Peter Watson, *From Manet to Manhattan* (New York, Random House, 1992).

Peter Watson, *Sotheby's: Inside Story* (London: Bloomsbury, 1997).

Einat Wilf, *Politics of Culture: International Disputes Over Ownership* (Cambridge: Harvard University Press, 1996).

Robert Wraight, *The Art Game* (New York: Simon and Schuster, 1966).

Periodicals:
Art Research News, New York: International Foundation for Art Research, 1981-.

IFAR Journal, New York: International Foundation for Art Research 1998-.

IFAR Reports, New York: International Foundation for Art Research, 1985-1998.

Stolen Art Alert, New York: R. R. Bowker Co., 1980-1984.

Index of Stolen Art. New York: International Foundation for Art Research, 1977-.

Afterward: Entarte Kunst

During my initial research about art theft, I received a number of questions from my colleagues regarding the Nazi's looting of Europe during World War II. Due to interest in this topic, I wrote a paper on the subject of Adolf Hitler's crusade against "degenerate art." The paper was published in Art Criticism in the Spring of 2002 under the title "Entarte Kunst." Given that this was where my research on art theft began and its tremendous impact on the modern art world, I thought it would be a fitting to end this book by reproducing this essay.

The Chiaroscuro Market

The week of July 18th, 1937 saw the opening of two major exhibits in Munich Germany. The first was the opening of The Great German Art Exhibition, which was the inaugural exhibition of the Haus der Deutschen Kunst. The second exhibition was *Entartete "Kunst,"* The Degenerate Art Exhibition. The two contrasting exhibitions, which faced each other on either sides of a public park, were a lesson for the German public. The first exhibition showed what art was acceptable, and in its presentation of idyllic nudes and victorious heroes it was also meant to show the public what it should strive to be. Across the park, the Degenerate Art exhibition was meant to show what was unacceptable. The works were laid out in such a way as to try to provoke their audience to hate what it saw. By giving Germany something to love and something to hate, the exhibitions were to unify the German people. They exemplify Adolf Hitler's use of art to rally support, to instruct the German people on who to be, and to fuel their hatred against those he created as enemies. However, the exhibitions were not solely propaganda, as Hitler genuinely sought to purify Germany of what he considered to be destructive forces. He saw modern art as a decline indicative of society's decline, and he wished to stop this decline by forcing art to adhere to what he perceived as principles it had contained at its zenith.

This paper will explore the development of art policy in Hitler's Germany, in order to set forth the methods Hitler used to remove the degenerate elements in German culture and to attempt to show that these methods, instead of being a cure, only further confirmed the decadence of their cultural position.

Before World War I, the German art world was in tune with the avant-garde. It supported the avant-garde through the 1920's with important exhibitions so that when Alfred Barr of New York's Museum of Modern Art visited in 1931, he was amazed at the innovative contemporary works already on display in Germany's museums.[138] The Nationalgalerie in Berlin had the most representative collection of contemporary art, though many local museums also showed works by German Expressionists. However, while there was an encouraging atmosphere for contemporary artists, there was also an opposition present. As early as 1914, there were passionate debates between conservatives and modern artists. In Prussia, these became political enough that the Parliament passed a resolution against the degeneration of art, though the resolution was little enforced as the question of degenerate art remained in the realm of opinion.[139]

Between World War I and World War II, Max Nordau's *Degeneration* of 1892 became popular reading in Germany. The work denigrated Tolstoy, Nietzche, Zola, and artists of a romantic nature as examples of social deterioration. In Nordau's eyes, nineteenth century realism was the culmination of tradition in the arts. The avant-garde became equated with the insane, being labeled antisocial for their hyper-individualism and their attempts to explore emotions. They were the unhealthy in art, as opposed to the tradition of empirical realism, and so the terms of "degenerate" and "healthy" came to be used to describe art.

A group of art philosophers built on Nordau's theme of the deterioration in modern art. Hans Guenther, in his *Race and Style*, declared that the Hellenistic image of

---

[138] Barr, Alfred, "Art in the Third Reich: Preview, 1933," *The Magazine of Art*, v. 38, October, 1945, 211-230.
[139] Nicholas, Lynn H., *The Rape of Europa*, New York: Alfred A. Knopf, 1994, 7.

beauty is absolutely Nordic. His book connected the style of an artist with that artist's race, art becoming a representation of man and his race. The consequence was that nineteenth century naturalism, which would become Hitler's favorite genre,[140] became associated with the Nordic, while Impressionism was de-Nordic because it accepted ugliness as reality.[141] Guenther defined the task of the Nordic race, the epitome of pure health in his eyes, as protecting itself from the degeneration of society indicated by the work of the avant-garde. The illness indexed by the avant-garde was also associated with Jewishness, as nineteenth century German psychiatry believed the Jew to be more susceptible to insanity and inherently degenerate.[142] Similar things were written by Ferdinand Clauss, and these ideas were later picked up by Hitler, who, in 1935, would state that the artist should never depict dirt for dirt's sake, or depict "cretins as representatives of manly strengths."[143] Instead, Hitler believed German artists should glorify the racial structures of their people.[144]

In 1928, Paul Schultze-Naumburg published his book *Art and Race*, in which figures painted by Impressionists and Expressionists were juxtaposed to photos of the diseased and deformed. Here, Guenther's connection between race and style became hereditary determinism; every being tried to continue the lineage of its kind and it used art to this end. What the artist portrayed was his con-

---

[140] It is interesting to note that for a time Hitler tried to utilize a slightly impressionistic technique in his own painting, though he was not able to go very far with this method. This fact may explain in some part his hateful attitude towards sketchy painting; his style could not progress past realism, and so he imposed this limitation on others. Zalampas, Sherree Owens, *Adolf Hitler: A Psychological Interpretation of His Views on Architecture, Art, and Music*, Bowling Green, OH: Bowling Green State University Popular Press, 1990, 29.
[141] Lehmann-Haupt, Hellmut, *Art Under a Dictatorship*, New York: Oxford University Press, 1954, 38.
[142] Barron, Stephanie, *"Degenerate Art:" The Fate of the Avant-Garde in Nazi Germany*, Los Angeles: Los Angeles County Museum of Art, 1991, 11.
[143] *The Speeches of Adolf Hitler*, edited by Norman Baynes, London: Oxford University Press, 1942, 578.
[144] Zalampas 86.

quering ethnic specimen. The art of "inferior" races deviated from the naturalism of Nordic art, just as that inferior
race has itself deviated from the healthy Nordic race, similar to Nordau's idea of degeneration. These thoughts cul-
minated in Alfred Rosenberg's *Myth of the Twentieth
Century* in which he characterized German Expressionism
as infantile and claimed that it was Nordics who built German cathedrals, Greek sculptures, and Italian Renaissance
masterpieces. One third of Rosenberg's text was devoted to
art's importance in society, and his synthesis of Guenther,
Clauss, and Schultze-Naumburg was popular, though he
would later find out at the Nuremberg trials that even the
high officials in the Reich had not read his texts very
closely.[145] Nonetheless, in 1933, soon after Hitler had been
made chancellor, Rosenberg was made "Custodian of the
Entire Intellectual and Spiritual Training and Education
of the Party and All Coordinate Associations."[146] Hitler's
support of Rosenberg stemmed from the importance he
placed on art to create a new mythology. This new mythology was partially a means to an end, a means by which a
totalitarian government could control the spirit of a
people. But it was also widely believed that the decaying
elements in culture were causing a cultural decline, and
these elements had to be exorcised.

Soon after Hitler became chancellor in 1933, he
passed a law that legalized the removal of all government
employees who did not obey the National Socialist ideas.
[147] This meant that many museum and gallery employees
were fired and replaced by those aligned with the party.
The new organization Reichskulturkammer would regulate
all non-government culture, with all artists being required
to join and no Jews or Communists being allowed to join.
Already, the famous persona in the Bauhaus had left and
Wilhelm Frick, as Minister of the Interior and Education,
had turned the institution into a German craft organization under Schultze-Naumburg's control. In addition,
films by Eisenstein, Brecht, and Pabst were banned.[148]
Frick had also begun to clear works by Paul Klee, Wassily

---

[145] Lehmann-Haupt 43.
[146] Nicholas 10.
[147] Ibid. 9.
[148] Zalampas 54.

Kandinsky, Emil Nolde, Franz Marc and others from the Schloss Museum in Berlin under the reasoning that they were Judeo-Bolshevik. Due to the conflict between the avant-garde and German nationalistic realism, the work of the avant-garde, with its complexity and inability to be readily understood, came to be seen as intellectual, elitist, and foreign by a nation demoralized by the effects of World War I. This was compounded by many artists' involvement in socialism during the Weimar era being communicated in their art so that more abstract works came to be identified with socialism and internationalism as opposed to nationalism.

In the 1920s, following the influence of Nordau and others, the German Art Association was founded to combat "corruption in art" and "promote pure German art," which did not include the progressive elements of the avant-garde.[149] Similarly, in 1927, the Combat League for German Culture was founded to fight for creativity that was thought to have been broken by foreign influence and was no longer able to attend to the demands of daily life. The seeds for the Munich exhibits were being set. The ideology of what would be acceptable had been arrived at through the writings of Nordau, Guenther, Clauss, Schultze-Naumburg, and Rosenberg. As Hitler became dictator in late 1933, it would be his taste combined with the developed ideology that would decide what was to be permitted. The false art was said to have been shaken off; from now on, there was to be no unfinished works, no pacifist works, no works depicting inferior races, the non-heroic, the Communist, or the Jew.[150] Art was to be used to give German culture a sense of strength, and in particularly, to help rebuild the notion of the German warrior. But to be clear, the attack of modernism was not just a device to gain support of the German people who had shown distrust in the new styles. This was certainly a consideration, but there was also the real belief that art reflected, and even determined, the moral life and value of the nation and its people.[151] If the "corruption" was allowed to exist, it was believed it would infect the essence of what it

---

[149] Barron 11.
[150] Ibid. 10.
[151] Zalampas, 54.

meant to be German. The Nazis had perceived that the modern world was pathological; it was not healthy for the individual. In *Mein Kampf*, Hitler had already written it was the business of the state to prevent people from being driven to madness by removing from culture "what is bad or unsuitable and continue building on the sound spot that has been laid bare."[152]

The period between 1933-1937 would be seen by Hitler as a four year grace period for artists, dealers, and those working in the arts to reform themselves to meet National Socialist standards of decency. However, the methods that he Nazi's planned to use to reform had already been experimented with during the last years of ideological consolidation. In 1930, the director of the Zwichau Museum was fined for "pursuing an artistic policy affronting the healthy folk feeling of Germany."[153] The Nationalgalerie was criticized for buying a van Gogh instead of German works. These protests were not connected with the Nazi movement, but after 1933 the Reichskulturkammer would use the resentment shown by these protests to their advantage. A director of another museum was fired for purchasing modern works, such as a Chagall. The works were paraded around the town on a truck with the picture of the director and how much he had paid for the work written on the side of the truck. Art dealers were also under observation; an exhibition of works by Franz Marc was said to endanger National Socialist Kultur Politic and public safety and order.[154] Many of the avant-garde chose to leave, and those who stayed were often not allowed to work and were subject to periodical surprise inspections by the Gestapo. They were not included in the production of a manifesto that Joseph Goebbels, Hitler's second in command, oversaw in 1933. The manifesto expressed what artists expected from their new government, but as it was written mostly by non-avant-garde artists who were angry that the art world had passed them by, it was an expression of party policy, stating that: one, all cosmopolitan and Bolshevik art should be removed, but

---

[152]Hitler, Adolf, *Mein Kampf*, translated by Ralph Manheim, Boston: Houghton Mifflin Co., 1971, 261.
[153] Nicholas 9.
[154] Ibid. 12.

first shown to the public who should be informed about its acquisition, and then the art should be burned. Two, all museum directors who wasted public money on "un-German" art should be fired. And three, there should be no Marxist or Bolshevik connections in the arts.[155] It became a time when opportunist artists who would kowtow to party policy could gain recognition and become successful while those who would not were in serious danger.

In the period between 1933 and 1937, the Nazi organizations in the arts began to consolidate, become organized, and gather energy. It was a four-year period of tightening the clamps that would end with Hitler's opening of the Haus der Deutschen Kunst in Munich, his temple of art. It was also to be the year of the Degenerate Art Exhibition, though this exhibition was to be the last and final exhibition of a type that had been maturing since 1933 with the help of the Combat League of German Culture. The first opened on April 4, 1933 in Mannheim, showing Images of Cultural Bolshevism Paintings. Works were shown not framed, with the purchase prices and dealers names noted next to the works. These, as one organizer said, were meant to be "documents of an age of decadence," publicly condemning the cultural policies of the Weimar system.[156] There was also a model gallery so that the Bolshevik works could be contrasted against what had been determined as good, Mannheim-based artists. Other tittles of German exhibitions in 1933 include "Art that Did Not Issue from Our Soul," "Art in the Service of Subversion," and the poetically named exhibition "Chamber of Horrors." Other exhibitions were meant simply to demonstrate the past art policy of the museum, showing prices for which pictures were purchased in order to arouse anger in the average German. There was also an exhibition entitled "Degenerate Art" that was first shown in Dresden in 1933 and toured Germany for the next three years. The exhibition included works by Grosz, Kirchner, Klee, Kandinsky, Kokoschka, Nolde, and many others. However, none of these exhibitions could compare in scale to the Degenerate Art Exhibition of 1937, in Munich.

---

[155] Barron 13.
[156] Ibid. 83.

The Degenerate Art Exhibition that opened on July 19 in Munich had begun to be planned only three weeks before. On the last day of June, Goebbels had authorized Adolf Ziegler, a painter of realist nudes and a member of the jury for the Great German Exhibition, to select and secure for an exhibition works of German degenerate art created since 1910. In the following months, Ziegler and his crew would acquire 15,997 works of art by 1,400 artists that were now deemed unacceptable and un-German.[157] 650 of these works would appear in the Degenerate Art Exhibition, including works by Georges Braque, Marc Chagall, Robert Delauney, Andre Derain, James Ensor, Paul Gauguin, Vincent van Gogh, Wassily Kaninsky, Fernand Leger, El Lissitzky, Edvard Munch, Pablo Picasso, Georges Rouault, and Maurice de Vlaminck.[158] Though Ziegler and his crew were supposed to pick post-1910 German works, many works predated 1910 or were by artists outside of Germany; however, this was later authorized after the fact by Goebbels.

Over the four months that it was on display in Munich, two million visitors past through the Degenerate Art exhibition, with another million visiting it during its following three year tour of Germany and Austria. This was five times as many visitors as would see the Great German Art Exhibition.[159]

Like previous exhibition of degenerate art, the Munich exhibition presented paintings without their frames, works being arranged in as cluttered a fashion as possible. The actual exhibition took place in a building that had been used to store plaster molds for the Institute of Archaeology. Pictures were hung as close to each other as possible, and stacked up to the ceiling. Next to each work was the tittle of the piece and its artist, with many works being misattributed. This information was handwritten, along with the year the work was bought and the price it was acquired for. There was no mention that these prices were in the post-war inflated mark, when one US dollar equaled 4.2 billion marks.[160] The astronomical prices of

---

[157] Zalampas 90.
[158] Nicholas 23.
[159] Barron 9.
[160] Ibid. 20.

the works were meant to enrage the public who was already suspicious of the avant-garde. There were also quotes on the wall from Hitler and others:

One thing is certain, under no circumstances will we allow the representatives of the decadence that lies behind us suddenly to emerge as the standard bearers of the future.[161]

We shall now wage inexorable war to eliminate the last elements of our cultural decay.[162]

All the artistic and cultural blather of Cubists, Futurists, Dadaists, and the like is neither sound in racial terms nor tolerable in national terms. It can be best regarded as the expression of a world view that freely admits that the dissolution of all existing ideas, all nations, and all races, their mixing and adulteration, is the loftiest goal of their intellectual creators and cliques of leaders.[163]

These passages were meant to help guide the visitor through the exhibition. Along with these quotes, some pieces were accompanied by short descriptions, for example:

This horror hung as a war memorial in the cathedral of Lubeck.

An insult to German womanhood.

The Ideal-cretin and whore.

Deliberate sabotage of national defense.

---

[161] Hitler at a rally in Nuremberg, 1933.
[162] Hitler at the opening of the Haus der Deutschen Kunst, 1937.
[163] Hitler at a conference in Nuremberg, 1934.

An insult to the German heroes of the Great War.

Nature as seen by a sick Mind.

Decadence exploited for literary and commercial purposes.[164]

And over one doorway it was written "They had four years." This short statement refers to the grace period given by Hitler for those in the cultural community to adjust to the Nazi way of thinking while Hitler put together his cultural machine. Those in the cultural community had been given four years to prove that their way of thinking was not degenerate or decadent in the eyes of the National Socialist party. From this point on, that which had not been proven as healthy would be eliminated. With the demonstration of the Degenerate Art exhibition and the Great German Art Exhibition, there was no room for an alternative view. Already, Goebbels had forbade art criticism:

> I granted German critics four years after our assumption of power to adapt themselves to National Socialist principles.... Since the year 1936 has passed without any satisfactory improvement in art criticism, I am herewith forbidding, from this day on, the conduct of art criticism as it has been practiced to date.... The art critic will be replaced by the art editor.... In the future only those art editors will be allowed to report on art who approach the task with an undefiled heart and National socialist convictions.[165]

To practice art criticism was to be critical of the art which was presented. And as only healthy art was to be presented, there would be no place for the art critic. What is more, to criticize the art that was presented was to be critical of the work that presented the ideals Hitler had set for the nation; therefore, to be critical of art was, by extension, to be critical of Hitler. Goebbels would continue to

---

[164] Commentary on wall of *Entartete Kunst*. Barron 49-80.
[165] Nicholas 16.

justify his ban on criticism through 1944, declaring that the ancients had disregarded art critics and had judged works for themselves.[166] However, the ban of criticism can also be seen as an attempt to mask the shallowness of a heavily censored art meant for mass consumption.

The Great German Art Exhibition was meant to underscore the official art's triumph over degenerate works as well as to demonstrate what the Haus der Deutschen Kunst would house. The building was to be the first of a new German artistic tradition, housing contemporary works to help further shape cultural policy. The exhibition opening was celebrated as a national holiday, German Art Day, with a festival and a parade of 3,000 costumed participants and 400 animals.[167] Hitler gave a speech on the contrast between modern ideals and German ideals with such passion that even his entourage were taken aback. He forbade artists to use anything but the forms seen in nature in their paintings. "We will, from now on, lead an unrelenting war of purification, an unrelenting war of extermination, against the elements which have displaced our art."[168] It was with these words that the audience made their way into the museum for the first time.

The 600 works that had been chosen for the opening were organized into categories such as landscape, portraiture, nudes, and military themes, with many works also focusing on themes of family, peasant life, and motherhood. So called art editors, having replaced art critics, reported in the press that "Sketchiness has been rigorously eliminated" and that the only paintings accepted were those "that are fully executed examples of their kind, and give no cause to ask what the artist might have meant to convey."[169]

The exhibition was straightforward, accessible to the point that it had clear messages without any room for interpretation. Such a message was conveyed by the many depiction of the Nordic nude, that, according to one report, "emanates delight in the healthy human body."[170] These pieces were instructional, embodying proper moral-

---

[166] Zalampas 70.
[167] Barron 18.
[168] Nicholas 20.
[169] Ibid.
[170] Ibid.

ity and behavior by symbolizing a standard of beauty and utilizing a classical vocabulary to avoid seeming sexual. They offered a moral standard around which Hitler hoped to unite a nation. This morality was represented in the bodies of the larger than life nudes that were smooth, and frozen so that they could be worshipped but not desired, like the Greece form.[171] In this way, beauty helped one maintain control of one's passions. And by depicting the nude in a static state like that of the Greek form, the works expressed unchanging values to those in search of values in post-war, modern Germany. The great statutes represented a link to Greco-Roman antiquity, echoing the tradition set forth by Rosenberg, a tradition of which the German people, hungry for national pride, could be proud.[172] The works suggested the greatness of those in the empire, while towering over the individual viewer, making him feel small and powerless against the empire.[173]

However, while the hushed whispers of the crowd generally admired the works for their realistic depiction of what was good and beautiful, the exhibition drew relatively low attendance, while the Degenerate Art exhibition drew record breaking crowds. Part of this may have been the aura of illicitness that the exhibition had.[174] No children were allowed and often times the doors had to be closed to prevent over crowding. And by drawing on the average German's distrust of the avant-garde, the exhibition gave the people what they wanted, an enemy to voice a unified hatred towards. The fact that the avant-garde was continually equated with Judeo-Bolshevik ideas and that the German public was voicing disapproval of the avant-garde helped consolidate the racism that Hitler was brewing. So not only was Hitler rewriting art history without the avant-garde, but he was also taking energy that was opposing the avant-garde and channeling it into his own racial-political agenda. The German people were uniting as what was acceptable and unacceptable was becoming clearer. Before the opening of the two opposing

---

[171] Barron 30.
[172] Zalampas 73.
[173] Redlich, Fredrick, *Hitler: Diagnosis of a Destructive Prophet,* New York: Oxford University Press, 1999, 122.
[174] Barron 84.

exhibits in Munich, it was often difficult to discern what was acceptable and what was not as there was no set criteria. Even during the shows, one artist had a work in the Degenerate Art Exhibition and one in the Great German Exhibition.[175] Arno Breker, the sculptor who was perhaps most fashionable in the National Socialist circles, had works that were confiscated. But despite this, the two exhibits served to take the ideas and theories of Nordau, Schultze-Naumburg, and Rosenberg, and make them into concrete realities that were understandable to all.

As should be apparent, a discussion of art under the Third Reich is impossible without discussing Hitler's attitude towards art. As the dominant personality of Nazi Germany, he imposed his ideas of art upon the nation. The two exhibitions discussed exemplify these ideas. He was deeply concerned with art, having made his living as a painter and having applied several times to art school. He saw art as a reflection of German culture, but also having the ability to determine the morality of a culture. He saw German art as decaying, and because of the importance he placed upon it, he wished to remove this decadence and replace it with art that contained the same elements contained in classical works and nineteenth century naturalist works, believing these to be the highest points in culture. In doing so, he was attempting to counter the decay. He had realized that the modern world did not help the individual, but instead of seeing art as a reflection of the modern world's disregard for the individual, he saw art as a catalyst for the destructive elements of the modern world. He saw modern art as unnatural and as degenerating progressively, and he desired to save his culture from death. But in doing so, he was fighting death, which would be the ultimate unnatural feat. Hitler distinguished German ideas form modern ideas, and wished to prop up traditional forms of expression that related traditional values so that they would resist time. He wished to fight time, and this is itself a sign of decadence: to continue to use methods after they have ceased to be innovative. Instead of encouraging new methods to blossom, he wished for artists to recycle old methods as they grew stale. The Degenerate Art exhibition was a removal of the new, a removal of progress;

---

[175] Ibid 18.

the Great German Art Exhibition was return to the old, an attempt to fight nature's law of death and to prolong the life of Hitler's idea of German culture.

After the Degenerate Art Exhibition in Munich, Hitler legalized the confiscation of degenerate art from state collections. This meant that the government did not have to compensate the collections for the work that was taken. This law was passed in August, after the Degenerate Art exhibition had been received by the public who agreed with its condemnations.[176] Hitler had waited to make sure the people agreed with the Nazi Party's actions before he claimed responsibility for them publicly. As expressed earlier, much of what the Degenerate Art exhibition did had been performed by previous exhibitions, though never on the same scale. It was this scale that gave the exhibition the resonance of a final declaration. The declaration having been made with the public's support, it became time to remove all the degenerate art from museums. Goebbels and Ziegler desired for this task to fall under their responsibility, though they received competition from Hermann Goering. It had been Goering who had ordered the close of the Bauhaus in 1933 and he had been using his power in the Nazi Party to gain power in the cultural administration. The dispute was settled by Hitler, who gave Goebbels charge of the degenerate art dealings, and instructed all party ministers to act more cooperatively.[177] This conflict was common as Hitler would often assign several departments jurisdiction over the same task, fostering a competitive atmosphere that not only ensured that tasks were completed, but that they were completed efficiently and often with more zealous than was necessary. There was also an ill-defined relationship between the Nazi Party and the government, due to overlap in function assignments and appointments and an unclear vertical chain of command. The result was all high personnel were dependent on Hitler for what they were to be doing; he was given last word in all decisions as it was clear he sat at the top of both hierarchies.[178]

---

[176] Petropoulos, Jonathan, *Art as Politics in the Third Reich*, Chapel Hill: The University of North Carolina Press, 1996, 60.
[177] Ibid. 62.
[178] Rodlich 104.

The following year saw an even more merciless attitude towards unacceptable art, with little regard for what the outside world thought. There were two main reasons for this: the clearance of non-German work out of Germany and personal gain. The purifying of Germany was always said to be the main reason for the Nazi's campaign against what they labeled as degenerate art, however, the desire to rid Germany of these works which were taken from collections without compensation presented a major opportunity for industrious Nazi officials. And it was not just individuals who would profit from the moving of art works, but the party itself.

In 1938, Ziegler's committee to find degenerate art for exhibition was transformed into a disposal commission under the control of Goebbels. It was then Goering's suggestion that Goebbels sell the degenerate works, which were greatly valued outside of Germany.[179] Goebbels approved of this idea and appointed three professional art dealers (Karl Haberstock, Karl Meder, and Max Taeuber) to sell the works in the Degenerate Art Exhibition. Soon, art buyers were approaching these dealers, sometimes because of the value of the works the Nazi's were selling, but also sometimes motivated by a desire to save these works from those who did not appreciate them and might destroy them. In some ways, the Nazi dealings operated like a ransoming. The works were taken from collections, if not by physical force, than by political force, without compensation. They were then held until it was known that the works were in danger. And finally, the works were sold to those who valued them.

Under Goebbels's authority, the organization of sales was begun even before the proper laws were in place. Goering, in an effort to cooperate with Goebbels, asked that thirteen Impressionist and Post-Impressionist works be placed under his authority. These works included Van Gogh's *Dr. Gachet* and Cezanne's *The Quarry*.[180] Through a complex series of legal agreements, these works were sent abroad and were used to obtain foreign currency and works by old masters that were more suitable to Nazi tastes. Each step of the exchange profited, Goering himself

---

[179] Petropoulos 77.
[180] Nicholas 23.

using money he obtained from the deal to purchase tapestries for his home. This personal gain was hidden by the simultaneous buying and selling of works for Hitler, which gave Goering the appearance of disposing of the works in a proper manner for the greater purity of Germany. It is also important to recognize that it was Goering's idea to sell the degenerate works, suggesting the he had plans to gain from their selling all along.

The selling of degenerate art by the Nazi party would last until 1942, with the war making art dealings increasingly difficult. Most of the capital that was accumulated through these sales went into special party accounts that could be used for arms purchases or to buy works aesthetically acceptable by party standards.[181] The biggest of these sales would be an auction that would take place at the Grand Hotel National in the Swiss town of Lucerne. Hitler's knowledge about these sales was substantial, as evident in his correspondence with Goebbels and his direct instructions to Goebbels on how to handle the sales.[182] After his tour of Italy in 1938, Hitler had realized that his collection would not suffice for his idea of what Germany's new museums should be.[183] German museums would need to expand their inventory by large leaps.

There were several ways of accomplishing this expansion. After Kristallnacht, the confiscation of art works from Jews was begun. Jews were forced to register their belongings, which made a convenient inventory list for organizations in charge of finding works of art. The confiscation of art works owned by Jews continued from 1938 until 1942. The confiscation process was aimed both at large collections, like those of the Rothschild family, and at single works of art owned by families with less wealth. According to policy, a family's property was not allowed to be confiscated until the family had left Germany, as leaving Germany was taken as abandonment of the property. But with authorities competing over the Jewish works, limits to policies were often overlooked. The confiscated

---

[181] Rodlich 123.
[182] Petropoulos 81.
[183] Nicholas 42.

property of 27 out of 59 Jewish families was of families who had not left Germany, or roughly half.[184]

Another source of works of art were the foreign territories Hitler's forces came to occupy. Special military units were formed to seek out works of art in battle torn areas and to then ship these works back to Germany. Experts were employed to "protect" works in war torn areas by finding valuable pieces in battle zones to be sent back to Berlin.[185] But there can be no question that these experts understood they were helping the Nazis find works to steal. The most valuable of these pieces were reserved for the Fuhrer's collection, or Fuhrervorbehalt, which came to be the same as the collection of Germany's state museums. Lesser works were taken by officials to decorate their offices or homes. An organization called the Vugesta evenly openly sold confiscated works in their possession to Nazi officers. [186] Though Goering would be successful in finding works for the Reich and for himself in Poland, the Baltic States, and South Tyrol, the real fertile territory was to be France. The traditional aesthetic of the Nazi's found many desirable works in occupied France, and the taking of these works, paired with the knowledge that they were being added to a rapidly growing national collection, would have exorcised a feeling of cultural inferiority that German leaders, including Hitler, might have felt towards France as the leader of Western culture.[187] This plundering was fueled by feelings of revenge over the injustices of the Versailles Treaty, as well as revenge for works of art that head been taken from Germany by Napoleon. This includes Jan van Eyck's *Ghent Altarpiece* and Dirk Bout's *Last Supper*, which were both high on Hitler's list of German pieces to obtain. In 1940, Goebbels was asked by Hitler to seize works lost in the Napoleonic Wars and to secure works of German origin and with German characteristics, criteria that was applied broadly. But Goebbels failed as a plunderer and was replaced by Rosenberg in 1940, who established several committees to assist in the appropriations. French Jewish art was confiscated, cata-

---

[184] Petropoulos 93.
[185] Ibid. 106.
[186] Ibid. 91.
[187] Ibid. 123.

logued in the Louvre, which had become a German art shipping depot, and sent to Germany. And, as with the rest of the Reich, there were multiple organizations vying for this loot, making the activity more energetic and fierce, with Goebbels, Rosenberg, and Joachim von Ribbentrop all leading looting committees. Yet Hitler remained the one who was able to determine the fate of the art, making all of the competing officers beholden to him and solidifying his power.

There was a great deal of work that was found in France, as in other areas, that did not reach the Nazi's standard of good German art. This work was sold or bartered like works from the Degenerate Art exhibition. However, the Nazi's lack of respect for the art worked against them, as they continually sold the work for prices far under the possible market value. For example, the Nationalgalerie sold Beckman's *Southern Coast* for $20, Kandinsky's *Ruhe,* now owned by the Guggenheim Museum in New York, for $100, and Kirchner's *Strassenzene,* now owned by MoMA in New York, for $160.[188] The prices show how eager the Nazi sellers were to get the works out of their possession. In November of 1941, the Degenerate Art Exhibition, which had been touring Germany and Austria, came to its thirteenth and last venue. At this time, only eight paintings, one sculpture, and thirty-two graphic works remained of the original exhibition.[189] The rest of the 650 works had been sold for foreign currency and replaced by confiscated works. Of the works for which Goebbels was responsible, 300 paintings and 3,000 graphic works were sold by between 1938 and 1941.[190] The attitude the Nazi sellers had towards modern art is with no doubt disrespectful, but they also paid it a compliment. The hurried pace with which they sought to get rid of the work suggests a fear of the art; their need to get rid of the art acknowledges that the art is powerful, and if their measures are an indication of their fear, then they most have thought the work to be some of the most powerful in history.

---

[188] Nicholas 25.
[189] Barron 95.
[190] Petropoulos 82.

But the exportation of undesirable works was only half of the task set forth by Hitler. The other half was the building of a national collection of pure German work that would make all other collections pale in comparison. Hitler dreamed of making his hometown of Linz the "German Budapest."[191] In 1941, just as the Linz project began with 497 paintings, Washington's National Gallery opened with 475. Fifty years later, the Washington National Gallery had 3,000 works of art. By 1945, Linz had 8,000 works, not including those of other affiliated agencies on which it could call at any time.[192] That is the an acquisition rate of five or six major works, such as by Vermeer, Durer, Holbein, Grunewald, Rembrandt, and Rubens, a day. Museums, like the one at Linz, were to demonstrate the greatness of Germany with monumental architecture containing the world's finest cultural artifacts which traced out German history in culture and made it seem the center of humanity and the model society.[193] The German public could go to these museums and understand where they came from and who they were supposed to be according to the ideology set forth by German art philosophers. The works they contained where to represent the ideal, the perfect Germany at its purist and healthiest, without being infested by degenerate or decadent elements.

Yet the behavior that was exhibited in the acquisition of these works ironically falls short of the healthy behavior that they were supposed to foster. Though authorities were careful to administer a net of laws that legalized any actions that they would undertake, the uncompensated acquisition of valuable works of art meets any definition of looting or plundering, an activity that would be hard to incorporate as a part of a healthy society. And the behavior of high officials, such as Goering, who took works for themselves for personal gain in secrecy and against regulations would suggest a degree of decadence in the official chain of command. Officers at most levels taking works for themselves that were expressly meant for other uses suggests a problem with the leadership structure. This is

---

[191] Nicholas 41.
[192] Ibid. 49.
[193] Rodlich 122.

supported by the leaders fierce competitiveness, flaunting of power, and disregard for regulations. These activities suggest an individual greediness that is also evident in the Nazi Party as a whole, attempting to occupy as much territory and acquire as much wealth as possible, using brutal and criminal tactics. And the violence of the military can also be seen in the methods commandos and Gestapo soldiers used to acquire works of art as well as to dispose of them. On March 20, 1939, in an effort to dispose of works that officials believed would not be worth trying to sell, 1,004 paintings and sculptures and 3,825 graphic works were burned in a bonfire in the courtyard of the Berlin Fire Department's headquarters.[194] Unlike the book burnings performed earlier, this act was performed in secrecy, which suggests that even those who organized the event felt it was something that should be hidden from public view. This exercise exemplifies the rage Hitler showed to the degenerate works, that he believed to cause moral decay in society. And yet this action was meant to be one of cleansing and purification.

I do not think it would be an exaggeration to say that Hitler feared the power degenerate art held over society, and that he felt compelled to rid Germany of this decay in order to defend its purity. However, he did not seek to understand the model of health that was the goal of the purification. This model of health was outdated and did not emerge from the contemporary situation. The attempt to stop what Hitler perceived as a decay of German culture is a decadent act, as it is an act meant to go against nature's progress by regressing. These behaviors exhibited by Hitler, as leader of the Nazi party, as well as the actions of the officials under him, suggest that the action they saw as the purification of Germany was as degenerate as any work of art of which they sought to rid themselves.

---

[194] Nicholas 25.